Steering Committee

Alvin Alm
President, Alliance Technologies Corporation

Gerald Barney
Director of the Institute of 21st Century Studies, Global Studies Center

Carl Blumstein
Managing Director, American Council for an Energy-Efficient Economy; Research Policy Analyst, Universitywide Energy Research Group, University of California

Roger Carlsmith
Director, Conservation and Renewable Energy Program, Oak Ridge National Laboratory

Jack M. Hollander
Vice President for Research and Graduate Studies, Ohio State University

John Sawhill
Director, McKinsey and Company

Robert H. Socolow
(Steering Committee Chair) Director, Center for Energy and Environmental Studies, Princeton University

Jon Veigel
President and Executive Director, North Carolina Alternative Energy Corporation

Task Group Members

W. Bradford Ashton
Program Manager, Battelle, Pacific Northwest Laboratories

Deborah Bleviss
Executive Director, International Institute for Energy Conservation

Harvey Brooks
Professor of Technology and Public Policy (Emeritus), Kennedy School of Government, Harvard University

Ralph Cavanagh
Senior Attorney, Natural Resources Defense Council

William U. Chandler
Consultant, American Council for an Energy-Efficient Economy, Senior Scientist, Battelle, Pacific Northwest Laboratories

Nicholas A. Fedoruk
Director, Energy Conservation Coalition

John Firor
Director, Advanced Study Program, National Center for Atmospheric Research

Howard S. Geller
Associate Director, American Council for an Energy-Efficient Economy

David Goldstein
Senior Scientist, Natural Resources Defense Council

Barbara Harwood
President BBH Enterprises, Inc.

David Potter
Vice President (retired), General Motors Corporation

Affiliations are listed for identification only.

Acknowledgment

*T*he authors gratefully acknowledge major contributions made to this report by many experts. *Energy Efficiency: A New Agenda* could not have been completed without the assistance of the Steering Committee and Task Group members. The Steering Committee provided valuable guidance and insight while allowing us considerable freedom. The task group contributed initial policy proposals, reviewed numerous drafts, and provided helpful comments. Among the task group, we are especially indebted to Deborah Bleviss and Marc Ross for generously providing advice and ideas. However, the authors made final decisions concerning the content of the Agenda and accept full responsibility for the final product.

In addition to the Steering Committee and Task Group members, we would like to thank specially the following persons for their comments on earlier drafts: Jan Beyea, Brent Blackwelder, Steve Brick, Bill Prindle, Paul Centolella, David Cohen, Gautam Dutt, Larry Frimerman, Charlette Geffen, Jack Gibbons, Holly Gwin, Jay Harris, Charles Hill, Ed Hillsman, Mark Hopkins, Carla Kish, Sean McDonald, Steve Morgan, David Moskovitz, Dick Ottinger, Michael Pertschuk, Ross Pultz, Bonnie Ram, Mike Reid, John Rivera, Harvey Sachs, Tom Secrest, Phil Sparks, Melissa Stanford, Allen Stayman, Tom Stoel, Michael Totten, Carol Werner, and Stephen Wiel.

David Sheridan provided skillful editing, Elizabeth Kellenbenz provided invaluable administrative support, and Emily Tynes contributed important production assistance.

Energy Efficiency: A New Agenda was made possible by a grant from John A. Harris, IV. Additional support was provided by Battelle, Pacific Northwest Laboratories and the John D. and Catherine T. MacArthur Foundation.

Table of Contents

Executive Summary

*T*hree major national priorities—environmental quality, economic competitiveness, and energy security—provide a new and urgent rationale for saving energy. None of these ends can be fully attained without also achieving an energy-efficient economy.

Energy efficiency offers U.S. leaders a practical means of achieving national goals. It protects the environment—in the short run by reducing acid rain and in the longer run by reducing the risk of global climate change. It strengthens U.S. security at a time when domestic oil production is declining and we are becoming excessively dependent on oil imports. Energy efficiency enhances the competitiveness of U.S. industries in world markets by reducing the cost of production, and serves the consumer by cutting lighting, cooling, and heating costs in homes and offices. It creates jobs and helps hold down interest rates. No energy supply option can provide all these benefits.

Energy efficiency works. It has permitted the United States to hold energy use to 1973 levels while expanding the economy by 40 percent. (See Figure 1.) Efficiency improvements now save the U.S. economy $160 billion per year. If the nation pursues energy efficiency aggressively and adopts the policies proposed here, the economy can continue to grow while energy use remains constant or declines.

New policies are needed because the United States is losing momentum in energy efficiency. Automobile fuel economy has leveled off after improving steadily for ten years. Industrial energy intensity, correcting for changes due to structural shifts, leveled off in 1983. Japan and West Germany now use only half as much energy to produce goods and services as the United States, making them more competitive in interna-

1

Figure 1: Energy Intensity Reductions, 1973-85

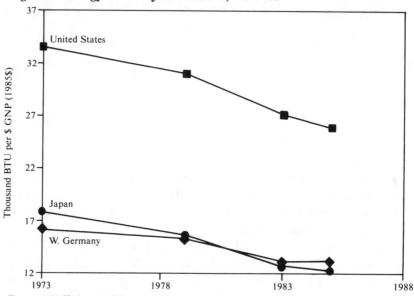

Energy Efficiency Works

Before 1973, most analysts thought that energy use and GNP moved together in lock-step. But energy demand has increased little since the early seventies, while GNP has grown by 40 percent. Energy-efficiency improvements now save the U.S. economy $160 billion annually.

Nevertheless, Japan and West Germany use half as much energy per unit of economic output as the United States. This fact gives those nations a competitive advantage.

SOURCE: *International Energy Agency*

tional markets. Oil prices have fallen below their real cost to society, causing U.S. oil imports to jump 35 percent since 1985.

To protect and enhance the U.S. environment, its economy, and its security, we urge the United States to place efficiency at the top of its energy agenda. *We propose that the nation set a goal of reducing energy intensity—the rate of energy used per dollar of economic output—by at least 2.5 percent per year well into the next century.* This rate would approximate the efficiency improvements of 1976-86, during which two oil price surges accelerated energy-efficiency improvements. It can be achieved using available, cost-effective technologies, which are often overlooked because of low energy prices and market imperfections.

This report describes six energy-efficiency policy initiatives—and twenty-one specific policy actions—critical to meeting the energy-efficiency goal. (See Table 1.) Our list is not meant to be all-inclusive, for other measures can supplement the effort. Specifically, we propose that the nation:

- Apply energy-efficiency to protect the national and global environment;
- Double car and light truck fuel economy to cut oil imports;
- Promote least-cost utility services;
- Enhance industrial competitiveness with energy-efficiency research;
- Make buildings more efficient to improve their affordability;
- Help developing countries acquire skills and technologies for energy efficiency.

These policy priorities have been selected for four reasons. They address problems that the marketplace cannot completely solve. They represent the largest of many opportunities to save energy and accomplish other objectives cost effectively. They ameliorate critical problems that energy use causes for the global environment, the economy, and national security. And they are compatible with ongoing efforts to reduce the federal deficit—indeed, the revenues generated in implementing these policies will far exceed expenditures.

We do not advocate saving energy as an end in itself. It makes sense only when saving energy costs less than providing energy, including environmental damage and security risks in the comparison. (See Figure 2.) Moreover, energy efficiency does not require sacrifice. The challenge is to use public policy in ways that complement the market, enabling the nation to realize the multiple benefits of greater energy efficiency.

Table 1. Policies for an Energy-Efficient Economy

Goal: Reduce U.S. energy intensity by 2.5% per year

Applying energy efficiency to protect the national and global environment

1. Reduce the risk of climatic change through an international energy-efficiency protocol.
2. Establish Soviet, American, and OECD cooperation to promote energy efficiency on a global basis.
3. Develop technologies that simultaneously save energy and protect the stratospheric ozone layer.
4. Use emissions ceilings for acid rain control.
5. Encourage integrated energy and environmental planning at the state and federal levels.

Doubling car and light truck fuel economy to cut oil imports

1. Raise gasoline and diesel fuels taxes by 10 cents per gallon for at least three consecutive years.
2. Raise car and light truck fuel economy standards to 45 and 35 mpg, respectively, by the year 2000.
3. Establish a gas-guzzler tax, gas-sipper rebate program.

Promoting least-cost utility services

1. Provide utilities with financial incentives to promote energy efficiency and least-cost energy services.
2. Allow energy-efficiency investments to compete with energy supply options in competitive bidding schemes.
3. Encourage least-cost planning through federal regulation of interstate power sales.
4. Conduct research and evaluation to improve utility, state, and local energy conservation programs.

Table 1: Continued

Enhancing industrial competitiveness with energy-efficiency research

1. Increase the commitment to federal energy-efficiency research and development and re-establish the federal role in demonstrating new energy-efficient technologies.
2. Establish research centers for energy-intensive industrial processes.
3. Establish a program to monitor and distribute information on foreign energy efficiency research.

Making buildings more efficient to improve their affordability

1. Improve the effectiveness of and increase funding for low-income weatherization, especially for multi-family buildings.
2. Establish federal minimum efficiency standards for fluorescent and incandescent lamps.
3. Improve the energy efficiency of federal buildings.
4. Expand federal technical assistance for conservation efforts.

Helping developing nations acquire skills and technology for energy efficiency

1. Modify the energy planning and lending policies of the World Bank and other multilateral lending and development institutions.
2. Provide technology and policy assistance for energy efficiency to developing countries through U.S. and other American agencies.

Figure 2: Cost of Energy Saved vs. Cost of Energy Supply

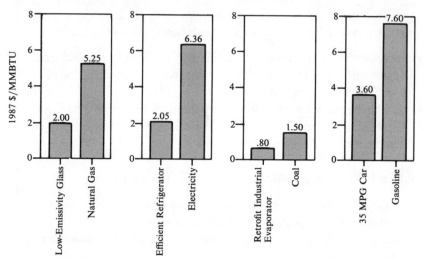

Energy Efficiency: The Cost Advantage

The cheapest way to satisfy growing demand for energy services is to invest in energy efficiency. Home insulation costs far less than nuclear or coal-fired electricity. Auto fuel economy can be built into new cars for less than the price of gasoline. Industrial retrofits save money even with today's low energy costs. The cost advantage shown above does not even count the environmental and national security benefits that energy efficiency inherently offers.

SOURCE: *American Council for an Energy-Efficient Economy*

How can energy efficiency protect the environment?

Unchecked fuel use could irrevocably alter the global environment. Atmospheric warming caused, in part, by the greenhouse effect of fossil fuel emissions could shift rainfall patterns and raise sea levels. The U.S. breadbasket could be turned into a dustbowl. East-coast beaches might be eroded forever, and forests could deteriorate rapidly. Evidence is mounting that these changes are already underway, but the world need not wait for proof—energy efficiency can greatly reduce the risk of climate change *and* it can be justified entirely on its own economic merits.

We propose that the United States sponsor the first and most important of a series of protocols to control greenhouse gas emissions: An agreement among nations to reduce the energy intensity of the world economy. This initiative would inaugurate an international process for setting and periodically modifying energy-efficiency goals and reporting on implementation plans. A reasonable and effective goal is to reduce global energy use per unit of economic output by roughly two percent per year for at least the next three decades. We suggest that the United States set an example by pursuing a goal of at least 2.5 percent per year. In conjunction with this agreement, *we propose a major cooperative effort among the United States, the Soviet Union, and other countries to share research and information on technologies for improving the efficiency of energy use.*

Acid rain is already seriously damaging forests, lakes, crops, and materials in the United States. Energy efficiency is not a complete solution to the acid rain problem, but it can significantly cut emissions and pollution control costs. *We propose that energy efficiency be applied to reduce the cost of acid rain cleanup for the nation.*

In addition, we suggest that *a research program be undertaken to develop technologies that simultaneously save energy, reduce greenhouse warming, and protect the stratospheric ozone layer.* Such technologies are needed to avoid increasing energy use when chlorofluorocarbon (CFC) production is reduced, as agreed by the United States and other nations in 1987.

How can the United States strengthen its energy security and reduce dependence on oil imports?

Cars and light trucks account for one-third of U.S. petroleum consumption. Raising their fuel economy is essential to reducing energy security risks. The technical and economic potential already exists to double light vehicle fuel economy. Doing so will help the United States prepare for declining domestic oil production, and help avoid putting the nation at the whim of foreign oil producers.

We propose a complementary set of policies to double automobile and light truck fuel economy. Economic incentives are needed to pull the market; performance standards are needed to push it. Specifically, a new transportation fuels tax is needed to more nearly reflect the real, long-run cost of consuming non-renewable oil resources. We suggest *increasing federal gasoline and diesel fuel taxes by 10 cents per gallon yearly for at least three years*. We also suggest *raising the fuel-economy standards for new cars and light trucks to 45 and 35 miles per gallon*, respectively, by the end of the next decade. In addition, we suggest *expanding the gas-guzzler tax and providing direct rebates to buyers of highly efficient cars* produced in North America.

How can the United States reduce the costs of utility services?

Utilities accounted for nearly 15 percent of total U.S. investment in new plant and equipment in recent years. Moderating growth in electricity and natural gas demand would lower this level of investment, thereby reducing the risk of over-building expensive power plant capacity and lowering the cost of capital. Likewise, cutting the cost of heat, light, refrigeration, and other energy services saves consumers money, and helps the United States become more competitive.

To reduce investment by utilities and the cost of their services, utility commissions should redesign financial incentives provided to utilities. Specifically, *state utility commissions should offer financial incentives to public utilities based on their achievements in providing utility services at the least cost*. We also recommend that efficiency investments be allowed to compete with supply options in competitive bidding schemes; that long-term interstate power sales be made consistent least-cost utility plans; and that federal support be provided for experiments and evaluation to improve efficiency programs.

Executive Summary

How can government support industry's efforts to become more competitive?

Although the U.S. is pre-eminent in basic science, it lags in bringing new technologies to market. And it has lost market shares both in traditional areas of strength such as steel and automobiles as well as in some high-tech fields. U.S. industry, however, has the opportunity to open new markets in energy-efficient products. Furthermore, energy represents a major cost for many industries, and U.S. manufacturers must cut production costs if it is to compete internationally. Government can cooperate with industry to research, develop, and demonstrate new energy-efficient products and more efficient processes.

We recommend a renewed federal government commitment to cooperate and share the cost with industry of researching, developing, and demonstrating energy-saving products and processes. Special attention should be devoted to new technologies that simultaneously cut energy use and provide other benefits such as improved quality and productivity. This cooperative effort can be conducted by expanding the U.S. Department of Energy's conservation research and development program. In addition, we propose that the federal government together with private industry *create research centers in energy-intensive industrial processes*. These centers would investigate common industrial processes such as metal casting or chemicals separation—key elements of the industrial infrastructure.

How can buildings be made more efficient and affordable?

Because home energy costs account for one-fifth of poor people's income, energy-efficiency improvements could help make housing affordable for millions of households in this country. And in commercial buildings, which account for 27 percent of all U.S. electricity use, myriad savings opportunities remain.

We propose to improve energy efficiency in buildings through new or expanded policy measures. First, *we suggest efficiency standards for lighting products*, along the lines of the national appliance efficiency

9

standards adopted in 1987. Second, *we recommend increasing funds for low-income housing weatherization programs.* We also recognize the difficulties this program has encountered and suggest ways of increasing its effectiveness. Third, *we urge the federal government to lead the way by substantially improving the energy efficiency of its own buildings.* Aggressive goals should be set and supported by special incentives, guidelines, and technical assistance and research.

How should the United States foster efficiency in the Third World?

The three-quarters of the world's population who live in developing countries account for only one-third of the world's energy use. Nonetheless, studies show that energy use in many developing countries is extremely inefficient. Adopting energy-saving technologies saves money and frees energy resources for other uses.

The United States has a major stake in the economic development of poor countries. Their growth means increased trade and jobs for the United States and repayment of foreign loans. Thus, the United States would benefit by speeding the transfer of technology and skills for saving energy to developing countries.

We propose exchange programs and assistance to develop lasting capabilities in energy efficiency among Third World engineers, industrial managers, and policymakers. We also recommend changes in the energy planning and lending policies of the World Bank and the other multilateral development institutions.

In sum, the United States possesses the technical ingenuity and institutions necessary to create an energy-efficient nation. But doing so requires political determination. Energy efficiency improvements will continue to slow in the absence of new leadership and coordinated national policies. By placing energy efficiency at the top of his energy agenda, the next President can help create a prosperous, secure, and environmentally-sound nation.

Energy Efficiency: A New Urgency

Reducing Risks

*E*nvironmental quality, economic competitiveness, and energy security provide a new and urgent rationale for saving energy. Environmental protection demands energy efficiency. Few human activities affect the natural environment more than energy use. And no recent environmental threat is more alarming than global atmospheric change. Concern is driven by new evidence that the global atmosphere may be heating up and by the speed with which a related atmospheric phenomenon—the "hole in the ozone"—appeared and expanded.[1]

If current trends in greenhouse gas emissions continue, the earth may heat up 1.5 to 4.5 degrees C over the pre-industrial average temperature by 2050.[2] Even warming at the low end of the range will alter the Earth's climate beyond that experienced during the past 10,000 years. The major grain-producing regions of the United States, the Soviet Union, and China could suffer from reduced rainfall. U.S. beaches on the East Coast could be destroyed. U.S. forests could retreat northward as drought-induced forest fires, pests, and reduced moisture make survival difficult. Sudden, unexpected shifts in ocean currents could greatly compound the expected increase in extreme weather.

Energy use is the principal factor driving climatic change today. At least three-fourths of the carbon which remains in the atmosphere each year originates in fossil fuel combustion.[3] Fortunately, energy-efficiency improvements can greatly slow the rate of warming over the next 100 years.[4]

The spread of acid rain damage adds to the importance of using energy more efficiently.[5] Acid rain is already costing the U.S. at least $10 billion per year in crop losses and materials damage, and the possibility of more serious damage cannot be dismissed lightly considering that half of West Germany's forests have been affected by air pollution.[6] Energy efficiency is not a complete solution to the acid rain problem, but it can significantly reduce emissions and pollution control costs.

Economic competitiveness also demands greater energy efficiency. Cutting energy costs in manufacturing would permit U.S. companies to produce goods more cheaply, making them, by definition, more competitive. Nevertheless, U.S. industry has not cut its energy intensity as quickly or as much as its trade competitors, especially Japan, West Germany, and the United Kingdom.[7]

The energy problem in U.S. manufacturing reflects the larger problem of slow growth in productivity. The productivity problem, however, cannot be solved solely by conserving energy.[8] In fact, innovation appears to occur more rapidly when new processes offer multiple advantages such as cutting labor or material costs, raising productivity across the board, or providing improved services.[9] Thus, developing energy-efficient industry requires developing manufacturing processes that are efficient in many ways.

The United States, because it is the world's largest buyer of imported oil, can do much to keep OPEC from regaining control of the world oil market. But when, as now, the United States allows oil imports to climb rapidly, it risks putting OPEC back in the driver's seat. When world oil demand exceeds four-fifths of world oil production capacity, prices can soar.[10] A round of rapid oil price increases could send the debt-burdened world—including the United States—into a serious economic tailspin. This possibility is exacerbated by poor prospects for increasing U.S. oil production, even if oil prices rebound.[11] By failing to control its demand for oil, in other words, the U.S. puts its own economy and the world's at risk.

The large U.S. trade deficit demands energy efficiency. Oil imports now account for about one-quarter of the U.S. merchandise trade deficit. (See Figure 3.) If government projections are correct, the annual U.S. oil import bill of about $40 billion could increase to as much as $100 billion per year by 2000.[12] Efficiency improvements can greatly cut this serious drain on our economy.

Energy efficiency also strengthens U.S. energy security—and national security. A handful of countries in the Middle East control over half of

Figure 3: Petroleum and the U.S. Trade Imbalance

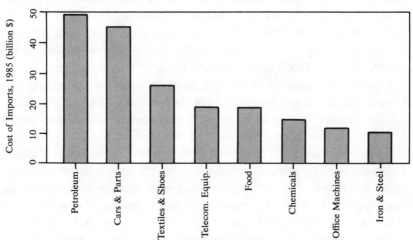

Oil Imports Account for One-Third of the U.S. Trade Deficit

   Oil imports contribute more to the U.S. trade deficit than any other single item. If government projections are correct, the annual U.S. oil import bill of about $40 billion could increase to as much as $100 billion by the year 2000.

SOURCE: *U.S. Department of Commerce*

the world's oil reserves. As the United States learned in the 1970s, its oil supply can be disrupted when it relies too heavily on oil imports from this volatile region.

Regaining Momentum

   The United States has made impressive gains in energy efficiency since the 1973 oil price shock. The nation has reduced energy intensity in every major energy-consuming sector. Industry has made the largest gains, cutting energy requirements per unit of output by 30 percent between 1973 and 1984.[13] Households cut energy use by about one-fifth over the same period, while owners and operators of commericial buildings cut energy use per square foot by more than one-tenth. The fuel economy of automobiles improved by 35 percent between 1973 and 1985.[14] Stringent national appliance efficiency standards were adopted in 1987 and will go into effect in the early 1990s. And the use of energy-efficient lighting products has proliferated in recent years.[15]

The country, however, is losing momentum in energy efficiency. The United States reduced energy use per dollar of output by an average of 2.7 percent per year between 1976-86. But the energy intensity of the U.S. economy dropped minimally in 1987, and an overall slowdown in efficiency improvements can be discerned in major energy end uses.[16] Industrial energy intensity, correcting for changes due to structural shifts, leveled off in 1983.[17] Automobile fuel economy also is leveling off. And light trucks, which now represent about 30 percent of new light duty vehicles, have exhibited almost no fuel economy gain since 1982.[18]

There are two main reasons for the slowdown in efficiency improvements. First, energy prices in general and the price of oil derivatives in particular have fallen in recent years. Corrected for inflation, the average price of gasoline in 1987 was nearly half that in 1980.[19] Natural gas and electricity prices have also fallen. The price-driven impetus for consumers and businesses to conserve has thus been diminished.

The other reason is that the federal government substantially reduced its commitment to energy conservation during the 1980s. Automobile fuel economy standards were rolled back; conservation research funding and federal support for state and local conservation programs were dramatically reduced; and implementation of national building and appliance efficiency standards was resisted by the Department of Energy.

U.S. leadership has failed to fill the policy vacuum formed by unstable energy prices. Today's energy market does not reflect the real national security, economic, and environmental costs associated with energy use, and government has not moved to correct this deficiency. Filling the void requires a reasonable goal for energy efficiency and a means of achieving it. *We recommend a goal of reducing the energy intensity of the U.S. economy by at least 2.5 percent per year well into the next century.* This will mean holding energy use constant or achieving a small decrease in total energy use by 2000 if the economy grows at 2 to 2.5 percent per year as now anticipated.

A 2.7 percent annual rate of reduction in energy intensity was achieved in the United States between 1976 and 1986. But the price shocks and many of the easier energy savings opportunities of the 1970s are gone. The U.S. Department of Energy forecasts relatively constant prices for coal and electricity, and only a 0.9 percent annual reduction in energy intensity through the year 2000.[20] Achieving at least a 2.5 percent annual rate of improvement well into the future will take political leadership and policies that will spur consumers, manufacturers, utilities, and other sectors of the economy.

Our efficiency goal is both technically achievable and economically justified. One study shows that it is technically and economically feasible to reduce the energy intensity of the U.S. economy even more—by 3.5 percent per year through 2020.[21] Our goal reflects a more cautious view regarding the speed at which institutional barriers and other limitations on implementation can be overcome, and the rate at which the building and equipment stock can be replaced.

Our 2.5 percent goal can be accomplished by: (1) learning from experience with energy policy; (2) supporting existing policies and programs that already are improving energy efficiency; and (3) adopting the new policy initiatives described in the next part of this report.

Aggressively pursuing energy efficiency has potential pitfalls that should be recognized and avoided. The federal government should avoid over-management and an overly short-term perspective. Close cooperation between government officials at all levels and the private sector is essential. Equity problems—among regions of the country as well as income groups—should be resolved, for example, when devising fuels taxes. Moreover, these concerns can and should be addressed by policymakers, not used to justify inaction.

Learning from Experience

Regaining momentum will require careful attention to what public policy can accomplish. The most important lesson gained from the energy policy experience of the past 15 years is that *energy conservation works*. Nothing has so dramatically improved the American energy situation as energy efficiency. The United States today uses little more energy than in 1973, yet produces 40 percent more goods and services. Efficiency has, in effect, cut the nation's annual energy bill by $160 billion. With little fanfare, efficiency improvements have become our most important energy resource.

Second, we have learned that *oil and natural gas price controls are counterproductive*. Energy price increases during the 1970s provided the basic impetus for the impressive U.S. conservation response. Two oil price shocks, oil and natural gas price deregulation, and escalating power plant construction costs each pushed up energy prices. Price increases helped to spark operating changes, technology improvements, and other conservation actions throughout the nation.

Third, we have proven that *technological ingenuity can substitute for energy*. A "quiet revolution" in technology has transformed energy use. Numerous efficient products and processes—appliances, lighting products, building techniques, automobiles, motor drives, and manufacturing techniques—have been developed and commercialized by private companies in the United States and other industrialized countries.[22] Energy productivity rose as more-efficient equipment and processes were incorporated into our building, vehicle and factory stock.

Fourth, we now know that *complementary policies work best*. Federal, state, and local agencies, including public utility commissions and the public utilities they regulate, have demonstrated the effectiveness of policies and programs that supplement price incentives and technology developments. Such initiatives helped overcome some of the barriers impeding greater investment in conservation—barriers such as lack of awareness and low priority among consumers; lack of investment capital; reluctance among some manufacturers to conduct research and to innovate; subsidies for energy production; and the problem of split incentives, exemplified by the building owner or landlord who does not pay the utility bills.[23]

Domestic appliances provide a good example of effective, complementary policies. First, the federal government established standardized test procedures, testing requirements, and a labeling program in the 1970s. Then, using these test ratings, states such as California and New York passed regulations prohibiting the sale of inefficient appliances. And these state efforts led to federal standards banning the production of less efficient models beginning in 1990. In addition, some utilities began

16

to offer rebate incentives to stimulate purchase of highly efficient appliances. Moreover, public agencies such as the U.S. Department of Energy and the Gas Research Institute supported the development and demonstration of innovative, efficient appliance technologies. These combined efforts along with rising energy prices led to a 25-80 percent improvement in the energy efficiency of new refrigerators, freezers, and air conditioners between 1972-86, with further improvements expected.[24]

Fifth, *conservation policies are not automatically successful.* A notable case of a poorly designed policy was the residential energy conservation tax credit. The credit proved to be the single most expensive federal conservation effort, yet little evidence exists to show the credit stimulated much additional conservation. Such incentives cannot easily be crafted to avoid rewarding consumers for actions they would take anyway as a consequence of price increases or to make homes more comfortable. And despite the large cost to the government, the subsidy was probably not large enough to induce substantial investments.[25] Similarly, the Residential Conservation Service and the Federal Energy Management Program did not provide sufficient incentives to encourage widespread energy-efficiency improvements.

Other policies have been highly successful, though. Without the automobile fuel economy improvements prompted in part by Corporate Average Fuel Economy Standards, fuel economy improvements would have been less impressive and U.S. automakers would have been less prepared to meet the surge in consumer demand for more efficient cars which arose after the oil shock of the late 1970s. Federal support for energy conservation research is another success, having contributed to the development and commercialization of numerous energy saving technologies during the past twelve years.[26]

Sixth, *the private sector is the primary vehicle for delivering efficiency improvements, but government-industry cooperation is essential.* Experience has taught that governments must work with the private sector to foster conservation actions. Private companies produce the cars, buildings, appliances, and machinery that use energy. They retrofit conservation measures in buildings and factories, and consume energy themselves. Research and development efforts aimed at new energy-efficient technologies or methods will only succeed—that is, end up penetrating the market—if private companies are directly involved in the research and development process. Likewise, program managers and policy-makers will benefit from involving equipment suppliers, builders, and retrofitters in the design and implementation of efficiency standards as well as conservation information, financing, and incentive programs.

Seven, *some utilities have learned how to benefit from conservation.* A growing number of utilities and regulatory agencies view demand-side management as a legitimate means of avoiding costly and risky energy supply investments. Consequently, utilities are increasingly investing in efficiency and load management measures, with total spending now at least $1 billion per year.[27]

And, eighth, *we have seen that political leadership matters.* Leadership from the federal government is essential. Federal programs can strengthen and reinforce the efforts of states, localities, private businesses, and consumers. Many conservation efforts, including fuel economy standards and research and development, work best at the federal level. Other efforts, such as utility regulation and incentive programs, work best at the state and local levels. Overall, a renewed commitment to energy efficiency is needed at every level of government in the United States.

Priority Policies

Applying Energy Efficiency to Protect the National and Global Environment

A concerted effort to accelerate energy efficiency is needed to reduce the magnitude and risk of climatic change, ozone depletion, acid rain, and major land impacts associated with energy use.[28] Energy supply alternatives to fossil fuels, unfortunately, cannot redress these problems soon enough. Nuclear power is too expensive and problematic. Renewable energy technologies are either too costly or can make only a small contribution to reducing these environmental problems over the next two decades. On the other hand, a multitude of energy-efficient technologies already exist, are highly cost effective, and can substantially reduce environmental damage.[29] These technologies can ease the transition to renewable energy sources.

Conservation of energy by itself cannot solve these major environmental problems; complementary efforts are necessary. For example, improved energy efficiency can only partly reduce sulfur emissions from burning coal; other sulfur control technologies such as scrubbers or clean generating technologies are still needed. Efforts must be undertaken to control other greenhouse gases and deforestation resulting from non-energy activities. But efficiency improvements will be most critical to reduce the risk of climatic change.[30]

Fossil fuel combustion produces three-fourths of the carbon emissions caused by mankind. These emissions along with other trace gases act like a blanket in the atmosphere to hold in heat. This greenhouse effect could produce rapid climatic changes and profoundly disrupt American forests, farms, coasts, and energy supply systems.[31] Traditional cultures in less-developed countries may be particularly affected because they do not have the means to adjust to changing rainfall and temperature pat-

Figure 4: Global Carbon Emissions and Energy Efficiency

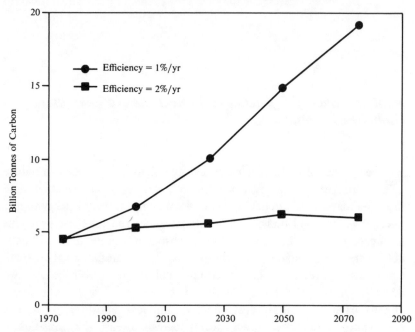

Energy efficiency: A Tool for Slowing Climatic Change

    The above cases show two future carbon emissions scenarios which differ only in their assumption for the global rate of energy-efficiency improvement. Relatively high economic growth would be permitted in either case. To achieve the higher efficiency scenario, implementation of policies such as those suggested in this document would be necessary.

SOURCE: W. Chandler, "Carbon Emissions Control Strategies: The Case of China," *forthcoming in* Climatic Change.

terns or rising sea levels.[32] Reducing energy consumption across-the-board offers the best hope to slow climatic change due to carbon emissions.[33] Efficiency gains would simultaneously slow climate change as well as reduce acid rain production, oil spills, and coal-mining impacts.

    Significantly, energy efficiency can be justified entirely on its economic merits.[34] This advantage makes efficiency both an effective and appealing strategy for averting global environmental problems. Because energy efficiency bolsters economic growth *and* offers an immediate, practical means of reducing the risk of environmental degradation, we urge the United States to lead a global initiative to promote energy efficiency.

Proposal: Reduce the risk of climatic change through an international energy-efficiency protocol.

This proposal would establish a process for an international protocol to reduce the energy intensity of the global economy. The process would have twin goals: reducing the risk of climatic change and promoting economic growth. The resulting protocol would produce an agreement to reduce global energy use per unit of economic output to a technically achievable and economically justifiable level by a specified date. By the year 2025, most countries should be able to reach the 1985 efficiency levels of Denmark, Switzerland, or Japan, which rank best today.[35] This level of efficiency can be accomplished with available technology and is justified at current energy prices.[36] It could be reached by continuing rates of energy-efficiency improvements experienced by many nations over the past 15 years. All nations, including less-developed countries, would achieve higher rates of economic growth by accelerating their rate of energy-efficiency improvement.

Discussions are needed to identify workable protocol criteria, promising areas for cooperation, and mechanisms for promoting compliance. The resulting agreement could establish energy-intensity reduction goals for individual nations, and provide for periodic review of the adequacy of goals and implementation plans. The United Nations Environment Programme offers an appropriate forum for these discussions.

While the agreement could involve different goals for different nations, we suggest a minimum 2 percent annual rate of reduction in energy intensity for the world as a whole. Twenty-one industrialized nations achieved this rate between 1973 and 1985, with the United States, Japan, and Belgium doing substantially better.[37] China has reduced energy intensity 3.7 percent per year since 1979, and plans to continue rates of intensity reduction greater than 2 percent.[38] Note that we propose a higher rate of intensity reduction—at least 2.5 percent per year—for the United States.

Certain nations that have both very low income and low energy-intensity levels could be exempted from the protocol. These nations typically have made little progress in the transition from traditional to commercial fuels. This category, however, does not include the most populous developing countries such as China, India, and Brazil which have large industrial sectors. Nations such as Japan and Switzerland, which are relatively efficient, could be expected to continue improvements over the period, but at a rate commensurate with the greater difficulty of gaining efficiency from an already low level of energy intensity. Additional issues such as the different climates of each country and trade in energy-intensive materials will require attention as an agreement is hammered out, but should not present insurmountable problems.

The Montreal Protocol On Substances That Deplete The Ozone Layer, signed by 38 countries in September, 1987, presents an important precedent for such an agreement. If fully implemented, this agreement could cut global emissions of chlorofluorocarbons (CFCs) by as much as 40 percent by the year 2009.[39] Like the proposed energy-efficiency accord, the Montreal Protocol represents an international effort to control a threat to the global environment based on long-term projections of environmental damage. An energy-efficiency protocol may be more difficult to achieve, though, because energy use pervades virtually every aspect of human life.

Implementing the proposed protocol would substantially reduce projected world energy demand, which some analysts expect to rise from roughly 300 quadrillion BTU at present to more than twice that amount by the year 2025.[40] Reducing energy intensity 2 percent per year would cut this growth by about two-thirds, saving 225 quads per year by the end of the period.[41] And as a result, global carbon dioxide emissions would be at least one-third lower than projected for 2025.

This achievement would increase economic well-being. Cutting energy intensity at the 2 percent rate could save world economies $500-750 billion in 2025, the equivalent of 5 percent of projected global economic output in that year. Econometric modelling results indicate that every region of the world, including the United States, would be richer with higher energy-efficiency levels.[42]

Proposal: Establish Soviet, American, and OECD cooperation to promote energy efficiency on a global basis.

An energy-efficiency protocol would establish efficiency goals and a means of encouraging compliance. A complementary component of international cooperation will be essential. Indeed, we consider energy efficiency in developing countries to be so important—for improving living standards as well as protecting the environment—that we deal with it separately, later in this report. Here we propose extensive Organisation for Economic Cooperation and Development (OECD) and Eastern Bloc collaboration to promote energy efficiency.

The countries would by formal agreement exchange scientists, industrial leaders, technicians, and students to promote the creation and use of energy-efficiency techniques in their own and other countries. The nations would sponsor both short and longer-term visits by qualified personnel to research institutes, universities, factories, and government agencies. The focus of these exchanges would be technologies for saving energy, means of fostering energy-efficiency policy, and the application of energy conservation to ameliorate environmental problems, particularly the greenhouse effect. The pervasive and decentralized nature of energy-efficiency techniques would offer the opportunity for many useful exchanges.

The United States has a long tradition of sponsoring scholarly exchanges with other nations in order to improve relations. The Fulbright scholarships program is the premier example. The United States and the Soviet Union first signed a bilateral agreement for exchanging scientific and technical personnel in 1954. During the Kennedy era, the Partners program sponsored exchanges with Latin American nations, setting up "sibling" universities between the United States and other nations of the Western Hemisphere. Many of these exchanges continue.

U.S. cooperation with West Europe and Japan and the newly-industrialized nations on the Pacific rim should be expanded, particularly in joint efforts involving cooperative research and information exchange on state-of-the-art conservation technologies. Precedents include the International Energy Agency agreement to share information and conduct joint research on heat pumps. The United States could benefit, for example, from learning about European advances in energy-efficient manufactured housing, or from collaborative research on the highly efficient Elred and Plasmasmelt steel-making techniques. Other promising areas for cooperation include building retrofit techniques, automotive technologies, and energy-intensive industrial processes. Cooperation with Eastern European countries could also be fruitful, for those nations are particularly inefficient and need capital and technology to reduce their energy intensity.

Proposal: Develop technologies that simultaneously save energy and protect the stratospheric ozone layer.

Chlorofluorocarbon (CFC) emissions deplete the stratospheric ozone layer shielding the earth from harmful ultraviolet radiation and contribute to greenhouse warming.[43] CFCs are important to energy conservation efforts because they are used as the working fluid in refrigeration and air conditioning equipment, and as the blowing agent in foam insulation. Roughly 40 percent of CFCs produced in the U.S. in 1985 was used in energy-related applications.[44]

Currently available substitutes for CFC-11 and CFC-12, the compounds which most seriously deplete ozone, are less energy efficient. For example, replacing CFC-12 in refrigerators or mobile air conditioners could result in a 10-20 percent increase in unit energy consumption. Replacing all uses of CFC-11 and CFC-12 with presently available substitutes could increase U.S. energy use by 4 percent.[45]

To avoid these energy penalties, we propose that the Department of Energy and the Environmental Protection Agency (EPA) undertake an urgent research, development, and demonstration program on promising technologies which could both reduce or eliminate CFC use and increase efficiency in energy-related applications. Some possibilities include:

- Evacuated panel insulation—highly insulating panels that could replace foam insulation.
- Alternative refrigeration systems and less damaging CFCs such as R-22 and R-134a.
- Advanced automotive glazing—improved windows and other techniques for reducing automotive air conditioning requirements.

Evacuated panel insulation appears promising because it requires no CFCs to produce and it could cut the electricity use of refrigerators and freezers by 25-50 percent. Although evacuated panels might add $75-100 to the initial cost of a refrigerator or freezer, net economic savings should total $300 or more over the life of the appliance due to large energy savings.[46] U.S. private companies are not developing evacuated panel insulation and some of the other options because they are technically unproven, highly novel, somewhat long range, and high risk. An intensive search is underway for direct CFC substitutes, but this research tends to overlook the potential for new systems—refrigeration cycles, insulation, and glazing, for example.

This critical research should be supported by a combination of federal and private funding. The effort would integrate and expand smaller, separate research projects on CFC substitutes and energy efficiency now conducted by federal agencies.

Proposal: Use emissions ceilings for acid rain control.

Acid rain, caused in large part by sulfur emissions from coal-fired power plants, now seriously affects many areas of the United States and Canada.[47] The most commonly proposed ways to reduce acid rain are to cut emissions by installing flue gas scrubbers, switching to low-sulfur coal, or using some of the "clean coal" technologies under development.

Opponents of acid rain control proposals have stalled legislation for years by arguing these control measures are too expensive. But acid rain control need not be expensive. In fact, a combined program of electricity conservation and acid rain control can yield cheaper electricity services (the cost of the electricity plus the cost of conservation measures) than if neither program were adopted.[48] Electricity services can be less expensive under the combined program for two reasons. Conservation programs that pay for themselves through energy savings reduce the demand for electricity, which reduces fuel consumption and emissions at power plants. And conservation programs can defer construction of expensive new power plants, saving more than enough money to pay for other control measures.

Unfortunately, many federal legislative proposals would discourage states from incorporating electricity conservation into their acid rain control programs because these proposals use statewide average emission rates to limit emissions. Statewide average emissions rates are calculated by summing a state's emissions from major pollution sources and dividing by fuel consumed at those sources. Statewide average emission rates discourage conservation because conservation can lead to reduced use of power plants whose emission rates are below the statewide average emission rate. This will cause the statewide average to rise, even though total emissions decrease. In other words, conservation-induced emissions reductions will move a state away, not toward, its emissions reduction target.

The problem can be avoided if federal acid rain legislation uses emissions ceilings instead of statewide average emission rates. Emissions ceilings simply impose a limit on the total tons of pollutants that can be emitted in a state. Thus, emissions reductions achieved through any measure, at any power plant, whether it be from conservation or direct pollution controls, will be fully credited toward a state's emission reduction goal.[49]

Combining ceilings with the least-cost approach to acid rain control and power supply could stimulate conservation and cut electricity use perhaps 10-20 percent over the next 15-20 years in states such as Indiana, Ohio, and West Virginia.[50] Over the same period of time, major acid rain-producing states could save $10-20 billion.

Some opponents of emissions ceilings have argued that ceilings may limit economic growth because they put a cap on total emissions. Rapid economic growth does not necessarily mean high growth in electricity demand, however. California has demonstrated that conservation programs can hold growth in electricity demand well below economic growth rates.[51] Furthermore, a wide variety of emissions control technologies are available for limiting emissions without constraining economic growth.

Proposal: Encourage integrated energy and environmental planning at the state and federal levels.

The functions of planning and managing energy conservation programs, energy supply facilities, and environmental protection in most states are housed in separate divisions and agencies. Environmental agencies, for example, regulate power plant emissions but are not involved in decisions regarding whether a new plant is needed and whether there are more cost-effective alternatives. Likewise, energy authorities order and approve conservation programs but usually do not consider the environmental impacts of energy production and use—as in coal surface mining, for example–or how greater efficiency can serve environmental objectives. Similar divisions exist at the Federal level.

Acid rain control is one area that could benefit greatly from integrated energy and environmental planning. Federal and state acid rain legislation could encourage state energy and environmental agencies to work together to consider efficiency improvements and least-cost utility strategies when developing statewide environmental protection plans. To promote such cooperation, federal acid rain legislation might include, for example, funding for the development of state least-cost utility plans. The EPA could provide grants to states for integrated planning, with states required to provide matching funds. If regional planning is appropriate, states could be permitted to pool their federal grants.

A few states already recognize the importance of integrated environmental and utility planning. In Wisconsin, the Department of Natural Resources and the Public Service Commission jointly developed a regulatory strategy for implementing the state's acid rain bill, and prepared a study of the potential to reduce compliance costs through efficiency improvements.[52] State officials in Wisconsin are strongly promoting electricity conservation, in part to reduce pollutant emissions.

Similar integrated planning recommendations and assistance could be of value for addressing pollution problems other than acid rain. Attainment of urban ozone standards, for example, has been extremely difficult in smog-prone areas such as Southern California. Improving vehicle fuel economy through efficiency standards or incentives should be considered as one strategy for meeting existing or tougher ozone and ozone precursor standards.

Doubling Car and Light Truck Fuel Economy to Cut Oil Imports

A growing gap between oil production and demand threatens U.S. energy security. If current trends continue, U.S. oil production will fall by one-third by the end of the 1990s—a drop from 9 to 6 million barrels of oil per day.[53] Meanwhile, U.S. demand for oil is growing rapidly again. As a result, oil imports have increased 35 percent between 1985 and 1987, from 4.3 to 5.8 million barrels per day. The Department of Energy projects that oil imports could reach 8 to 12 million barrels per day by the end of the 1990s, with an annual import bill of $100 billion.[54]

Vehicle fuel economy ranks first in priority for reducing oil imports. Cars and light trucks account for the largest share of U.S. oil use—fully one-third, a volume equal to imports.[55] Even though the fuel economy of cars has improved since the 1973 oil crisis, many opportunities for improving automobile fuel efficiency and performance remain to be implemented.[56]

The 1973 oil crisis awakened American interest in automobile fuel economy. Consumers demanded more fuel-efficient cars faster than the U.S. automakers could supply them. And in 1975, the U.S. government passed its most effective and forward-looking energy legislation, the Energy Policy and Conservation Act (EPCA), which required new car fleets to obtain an average 27.5 mpg by 1985. The EPCA standards, though recently reduced to 26 mpg, helped sustain momentum in fuel efficiency even after the oil price collapse of the early 1980s. In fact, fuel economy improvements in the U.S. light vehicle fleet since enactment of the fuel economy standards contributed about one-fifth of all the oil savings achieved by OECD countries after 1973.[57]

The technical and economic potential for again doubling fuel economy of cars and light trucks already exists.[58] The electronics revolution has made possible the use of sensors and microprocessors for more precise engine control. New transmissions will be able to continuously shift the gear ratio to match the most-efficient engine speed with the desired speed of the wheels. Though it would work at first only for small cars, this continuously variable transmission would provide a smoother ride and improve fuel economy about 12 percent. Numerous other fuel saving technologies could help double auto fuel economy.[59] (See Table 2.)

28

Table 2. Technologies for Automobile Fuel Economy Improvements

Technology	Percentage Gain in Fuel Economy by Mid-1990s
New Engine Designs (e.g., improved shape of combustion chamber)	4
Variable Valve Timing	8
4 Valves Per Cylinder	8
Multi-point Fuel Injection	7
Improved Lubricants and Friction Reducing Materials	4–5
Electronic Transmission Control	3
Continuously Variable Transmission	12
Improved Tires	5
Improved Aerodynamics	5
Efficient Accessories	2

Note: Percentage gains are not additive.

SOURCE: *Energy and Environmental Analysis, "Analysis of the Capabilities of Domestic Auto Manufacturers to Improve CAFE," 1986.*

A major barrier to the introduction of these new technologies is first cost. Cars twice as efficient as the current generation of cars will cost perhaps $200-800 more.[60] And though this first cost would be more than recovered through fuel savings over the life of the car, manufacturers probably will not install features if consumers will balk at their added cost at the time of purchase.[61] On the other hand, some innovations will both save fuel and cut manufacturing costs.

Accomplishing the goal of doubling fuel economy will require bold new policy initiatives. We have examined the effectiveness of a fuels tax, an oil import fee, a gas-guzzler tax, and fuel economy standards as means of doubling automobile fuel economy. We conclude that no single approach can accomplish the desired improvements in fuel economy. Raising gasoline and diesel taxes high enough to stimulate demand for 45 mpg cars would be politically difficult. Enforcing fuel economy standards in the absence of economic incentives such as rebates would also present problems. We therefore recommend a complementary set of policies that will both push and pull the market.

Proposal: Raise gasoline and diesel fuel taxes by 10 cents per gallon for at least three consecutive years.

The market price for imported oil does not reflect its real cost to the U.S. economy. Some studies estimate that the national security cost of importing oil amounts to at least $10 per barrel.[62] The costs of air pollution and the risks of climate change from using oil make the real costs even higher.

Logically, these costs should be internalized through a tax on oil regardless of where it is used in the economy. A tax on transportation fuels, however, would be more practical. The potential for increasing the efficiency of oil use in the transportation sector is large. Taxes on transportation fuels would cause fewer problems for competitiveness and employment than taxes in other sectors. Moreover, the collection mechanism is already in place for a new tax on gasoline and diesel fuel.

Thus, we propose a tax on vehicle fuels sufficient to capture a portion of the long-run costs of high oil use, coupled with rebates for low-income persons. Specifically, we urge the application of a tax on gasoline and diesel equal to 10 cents per gallon beginning in 1990. If world oil prices remain low (under $30 per barrel), the tax should be increased 10 cents each year until it reaches a maximum 50 cents per gallon. If oil prices rise substantially higher, the tax should be increased 10 cents each year to a

Figure 5: *Gasoline Price Levels, Selected Countries, 1987*

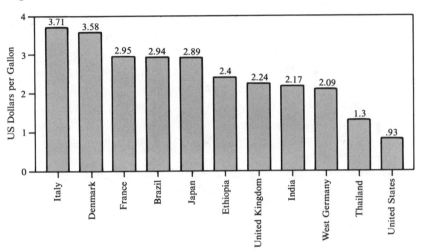

Foreign nations tax gasoline heavily, encouraging efficiency

Gasoline in Italy and Denmark costs four times as much as in the United States. This difference is due almost entirely to differences in gasoline tax levels. Low U.S. gasoline prices encourage consumption and place the nation at risk of new oil supply disruptions, price hikes, and reduced flexibility in foreign policy.

SOURCE: International Energy Annual, *1986 Energy Information Administration, U.S. Department of Energy, October, 1987.*

maximum of 30 cents per gallon. The intent of such a tax structure is to make the tax responsive to market changes so that whatever happens, consumers are given a price signal that better reflects the real cost of the resource and encourages conservation.

Precedents abound for taxing fuel to reduce its consumption. The price of gasoline at the pump in countries as diverse as Japan, Italy, and Brazil is two to four times that in the United States, mainly because of tax policy.[63] (See Figure 5.) The United States also has imposed gasoline taxes, both at the federal and state level. Generally, the intent of such taxes has been to raise revenues to pay for road construction and repair rather than to strengthen national energy security or some other national goal. The current average combined federal, state, and local gasoline tax is only 30 cents per gallon in the United States.

A fuels tax will have the major drawback of adversely affecting low-income people since they spend a disproportionate fraction of their income on energy. A portion of the tax collected could be rebated to low-income households. Many mechanisms for rebating the tax are already in place. For the working poor or retired persons, the income tax and social security systems could be used. For those not paying taxes or receiving social security benefits, other mechanisms such as aid to families with dependent children and public housing subsidies could be used to offset the tax increase.

The federal budget deficit demands reduction and may provide impetus for enacting a fuel tax. A 30-50 cent tax in the year 1995 would generate about $40-60 billion in revenues, and even after rebates to the poor, would provide significant new sources of revenue to the government.[65] Part of the revenue could be used to continue filling and perhaps expand the Strategic Petroleum Reserve, fund other energy conservation programs, or support maintenance of roads, bridges, and other elements of the U.S. transportation infrastructure.

Proposal: Raise car and light truck fuel economy standards to 45 and 35 mpg, respectively, by the year 2000.

Fuel efficiency regulations will be essential to capture the full potential of automobile and light truck fuel economy. The incremental savings attributable to fuel economy levels above 30 mpg are small compared to the total cost of owning and operating a car.[66] Moreover, it may take auto manufacturers years to respond to anticipated fuel price increases in the 1990s.

We propose that the government require new passenger cars and light trucks to obtain, on average, 45 and 35 mpg, respectively, by the year 2000. Interim standards should also be set. The penalty for failing to meet the standards would be a substantial tax on the manufacturers, based on the number of vehicles failing to meet the requirement and the amount of the shortfall. This approach differs from the original legislation which placed manufacturers in violation of the law for failing to meet standards.

We emphasize that light trucks are a high priority for fuel-economy policy. Purchases of light trucks have grown at an annual rate of over 6 percent during the 1980s. Most people now use these trucks as they would cars—for commuting, running errands, and recreation. As a result, the fraction of total gasoline consumption attributable to light trucks over their lifetimes is climbing toward 50 percent. Present law, however, requires that light trucks attain an average of only about 20 mpg. Light truck fuel economy could be increased with the same technologies available for improving the fuel efficiency of cars.

The proposed legislation would provide an opportunity to correct certain flaws in the original Energy Policy and Conservation Act. By setting an industry-wide standard that all manufacturers had to meet, the law discriminated against mainly American, full-line manufacturers that produced a range of car models, in favor of mainly Japanese automakers that produced mostly small cars. Annual increases in the fuel economy standards proved particularly burdensome because manufacturers do not change model lines nearly so frequently.

Careful structuring of new fuel economy standards could avoid these and other problems of fairness. The standards could, for example, require the same percentage increase in fuel economy for each manufacturer, or a fuel efficiency level based on interior volume.[67] We recommend that the final formula be established only after careful analysis and discussions with the auto industry to minimize unintended effects.

Opponents of fuel economy standards have argued that the standards reduce automobile safety.[68] But this need not be so. The United States doubled new car fuel economy since 1975 while cutting traffic fatalities per mile by one-third. Had fatality rates continued at 1975 levels, an estimated 17,000 more persons would be dying each year on American roads. The reduced fatalities came about in part due to lower speed limits and the crack-down on drunk driving, but better safety design also contributed. The 2,000 pound Volkswagen Rabbit, for instance, has a better safety record than the Chevrolet Impala and Ford Crown Victoria, which weigh almost twice as much.[69]

Additional auto safety improvements are possible without compromis-

33

ing fuel economy. For example, installing air bags or automatic seat belts in all cars and light trucks would avoid an estimated 12,000 deaths annually. Improved protection against side collisions could save over 4,000 lives per year. The key issue for safety—as it is for fuel economy—is design.[70]

Proposal: Establish a gas-guzzler tax, gas-sipper rebate program.

The fuels tax and fuel economy standards would raise average fuel efficiency, but would not address two important problems. The first is the need to discourage production of very inefficient cars and trucks—gas guzzlers—and the second is the need to encourage the production of highly efficient vehicles. A gas-guzzler tax would address the first problem; a rebate mechanism would address the second.

Since high fuel economy levels do not greatly reduce the costs of driving, U.S. manufacturers face a high barrier to fuel economy innovation. Manufacturers thus run considerable risks with innovative vehicles and have little prospect for rewards in the marketplace.

To help assure a market for super high-efficiency cars, we propose that a rebate like those offered by car dealers in promotional campaigns—on the order of $1000—be offered to consumers purchasing high-efficiency vehicles. The rebate would be paid by the federal government, using revenue collected through the gas guzzler tax. Manufacturers could qualify a limited number of vehicle models for the rebate by producing cars that meet a specified level of fuel economy, such as 50 percent higher than the most efficient models now available, and other important criteria, such as safety and low emissions. Different fuel-economy criteria could be set for different size classes of cars, and eligibility would be limited to models produced in significant quantities. Eligibility might be restricted to cars manufactured primarily in North America, but it should not be restricted only to U.S.-owned firms.

In addition, the existing gas-guzzler tax ought to be modified. The current tax mainly affects extremely inefficient luxury cars. A new tax schedule should be adopted that applies to vehicles with higher levels of fuel economy than presently covered by the tax. Tax levels in the schedule need to be increased, too. The combination of changes in the tax schedule and level should be sufficient to generate at least enough new revenue to fund the gas-sipper rebate program.

Together, these proposals can lead to oil savings of approximately 1.0 to 1.5 million barrels of oil per day by the end of the century. Such savings would cut U.S. oil imports in 2000 by 10-15 percent and would directly cut the import bill by $9-16 billion, based on government forecasts of future energy supplies and prices.[71] Furthermore, the savings represent 20-30 percent of the anticipated increase in oil use in all countries outside the Soviet Union, Eastern Europe, and China between 1985-2000.[72] A successful effort to raise vehicle fuel economy would significantly reduce pressure on world oil markets.

Promoting Least-Cost Utility Services

Energy supply facilities such as power plants and transmission lines are highly capital intensive. During the late 1970s and early 1980s, utilities accounted for nearly 15 percent of all investment in new plant and equipment in the United States.

Utilities absorb more capital than any sector of the economy other than real estate. And some utility supply investments—recently completed nuclear power plants, for example—have turned out to be financial disasters. Increasing efficiency reduces the need for investment in energy supply, which reduces the risk of wasteful power supply investments. It also frees capital for investment elsewhere, for example in industrial modernization. Efficiency improvements are helping the utility industry cut its capital expenditures from $50 billion in 1982 to around $17 billion per year expected by 1990.[73]

A least-cost utility services approach has emerged in recent years as a means for reducing capital investments in the power sector. The objective is to provide services such as heat, light, refrigeration, and motor power—not energy per se—at the lowest possible cost.[74] For meeting new needs for power, a kilowatt-hour saved from waste is indistinguishable from a kilowatt-hour delivered by a new power plant.

Under the least-cost utility services approach, all feasible conservation and other "demand-side" resources are evaluated along with new energy supply options and are ranked according to cost effectiveness. Since

Figure 6: Least-Cost Planning in the Pacific Northwest

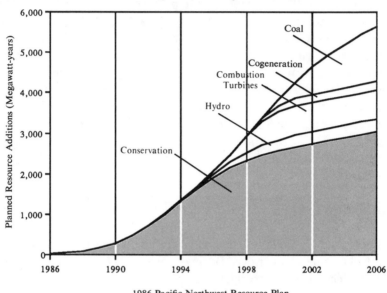

1986 Pacific Northwest Resource Plan,
Medium-High Case

Least-Cost Planning in the Pacific Northwest

The Pacific Northwest Power Planning Council thoroughly analyzes supply and demand-side electrical resources. It developed least-cost power plans in 1983 and 1986. Utilities in the region have acquired the capability to implement efficiency measures in order to avoid constructing numerous costly power plants, should the need arise. If population and economic activity grow moderately, the most recent plan calls for cutting electricity use 13 percent by 2006 at an average cost of about 2 cents per kilowatt-hour.

SOURCE: "1986 Northwest Conservation and Electric Power Plan," Northwest Power Planning Council, Portland, OR, 1986

energy-efficiency measures typically cost less than generating or purchasing a commensurate amount of energy, investing in efficiency becomes a top priority for utilities using this approach. And when flexibility, safety, environmental impacts, and social concerns are included in the analysis, efficiency looks even more attractive.

The least-cost approach was first adopted in 1980 in the Pacific Northwest.[75] (See Figure 6.) Since then, at least 16 states have adopted least-cost planning policies and requirements.[76] Some utilities have demonstrated that they can significantly reduce load growth in a cost-effective manner. For example, the Austin, Texas, municipal utility, Northern States Power Company, and Southern California Edison Company have been able to reduce electricity use and peak demand by 0.4 to 1.4 percent per year by offering rebate incentives to purchasers of efficient appliances and other equipment. This represents a 20-40 percent reduction in the rate of electric load growth. Utilities with rebate programs are paying only $200 to $300 per kilowatt saved, thereby acquiring savings at a fraction of the cost of new power supplies.[77]

But the least-cost approach to providing energy services is still not routine in the utility industry. Only a handful of utilities are committing more than a few percent of their total budget to conservation and load management. The majority is still encouraging load growth.[78] Furthermore, some forecasts predict or call for rapidly increasing investment in power supply facilities during the 1990s in order to avoid shortages of electric generating capacity.[79] This strategy could be very costly and risky, and it could result in utilities once again absorbing large amounts of investment capital.

The proposals in this section are intended to enhance economic growth and competitiveness by advancing the United States toward least-cost energy services, to increase support among utilities for energy efficiency, and to strengthen their ability to implement effective conservation programs. The proposals are addressed to the U.S. Department of Energy (DOE) and the Federal Energy Regulatory Commission (FERC) as well as to state officials and utilities. Electricity is the main focus, but a number of the proposals also apply to gas utilities.

Proposal: Provide utilities with financial incentives to promote energy efficiency and least-cost energy services.

Regulators should encourage utilities to pursue least-cost energy services by linking a utility's profitability to its progress in acquiring cost-effective sources of generating capacity and end-use efficiency. Utility commissions should also abandon ratemaking procedures that financially reward utilities for increasing short-run sales of electricity and gas.

Financial incentives and penalties could take a number of forms. For example, if a utility performs well in acquiring conservation resources, it may be appropriate to increase that utility's rate of return or earnings. If, on the other hand, a utility performs poorly in acquiring conservation resources, regulators could penalize the utility by lowering its allowed rate of return. Establishing performance-based incentives will safeguard consumers from paying for ineffective or overly expensive conservation, load management, and alternative generation programs. Regulators could base incentives (or penalties) on the amount of savings achieved, the cost effectiveness of conservation programs, or on a utility's ability to reduce the total energy bill of its customers.

A few state utility commissions have used incentives and penalties and rate adjustments along the lines suggested here. In 1979, the California utility commission penalized Pacific Gas & Electric Company (PG&E) for failing to make reasonable efforts towards developing the cogeneration potential in its service territory.[80] PG&E subsequently contracted for large amounts of cogeneration and independent power. The Massachusetts utility commission reduced the allowed rate of return for Boston Edison Company (BECO) in 1986 because of its poor record in developing and implementing conservation and load management programs and performing integrated planning.[81] Since then, BECO has established or expanded about 20 demand-side management programs.[82] Also, Wisconsin is using performance-based incentives as part of its effort to stimulate much larger and more effective conservation programs among its utilities.[83]

Adjusting electricity and gas rates provides another means of encouraging efficiency. Utility rates are usually based on near-term projections of electricity and gas sales. Utilities generally profit if sales are greater than projected in the last ratemaking case. This situation can be avoided by periodically adjusting rates so that profits are decoupled from fluctuations in sales volume. The California utility commission has established such a revenue adjustment mechanism.[84] State commissions could go even further by increasing or decreasing a utility's revenues and profits in proportion to the degree it is able to lower sales or energy service costs.[85]

Giving utilities a financial stake in encouraging cost-effective efficiency improvements is not without difficulties. Some states reward utilities for conservation program expenditures rather than for achieving energy savings or lower service costs. Paying incentives based on program expenditures is much easier but is far less desirable than incentives based on performance. Experimentation and careful evaluation will be required if incentives are going to be based on conservation program performance or a utility's overall progress in reducing customers' bills.

The federal government can assist state utility commissions in addressing these problems. We propose that DOE analyze alternative incentive schemes, including conducting case studies of recent initiatives through its Least-Cost Utility Planning project. Also, DOE or FERC could provide recommendations to states on how to structure incentive schemes and disseminate information on emerging least-cost strategies.

Proposal: Allow energy-efficiency investments to compete with energy supply options in competitive bidding schemes.

Providing utilities with incentives for pursuing least-cost energy services encourages comparison of energy supply and conservation options. A parallel strategy would allow energy conservation projects to compete with new energy supply projects through bidding procedures. This form of market testing would aid utilities in developing least-cost plans.

In early 1988, FERC proposed new regulations to stimulate greater competition in new power generation by allowing non-utility sources of energy such as cogeneration projects to bid competitively for rights to provide power to utilities. But FERC devoted minimal attention to the role that conservation projects could play in meeting resource needs at least cost. We propose that FERC remedy this shortcoming by directing or encouraging states to allow conservation projects to compete with proposals for additional generating resources.

Utilities in both Maine and Massachusetts have solicited bids for electricity savings.[86] Central Maine Power is paying 1 to 2 cents per kilowatt-hour saved in response to its pilot demand-side bidding program.[87] The utility offers to pay up to 50 percent of the initial cost for conservation projects in order to shorten the payback period to two years. Actual payments depend on measured savings. Conservation projects implemented through this program include installation of efficient motors by a wood products manufacturer and installation of an energy management system at a college. In late 1987, Central Maine Power received approval to allow supply and efficiency projects to compete directly.

Because there has been limited experience with conservation bidding and because there are a number of questions concerning how it would work, it is essential to experiment with the concept and carefully monitor impacts. Utilities must establish methods for determining savings, minimizing transaction costs, and maximizing program impacts. Also, special efforts are likely to be needed if demand-side bidding is to elicit conservation in hard-to-reach markets such as low-income and multi-family housing. DOE and FERC should assist states and utilities by evaluating demand-side bidding experiments and pilot programs and by disseminating information to further this concept.[88]

Proposal: Encourage least-cost planning through federal regulation of interstate power sales.

FERC regulates interstate power transfers which account for approximately 30 percent of U.S. electricity sales. We propose that FERC require buyers and sellers of electricity to demonstrate that proposed long-term power sales be consistent with either least-cost plans for the region involved, or with least-cost planning principles where such plans are not available. Adoption of regional plans would be encouraged by creating expedited approval processes for transactions covered by the plans. An amendment to the Federal Power Act may be needed to adopt this policy because FERC has refused to review proposed power transfers on the basis of environmental or least-cost impacts.[89]

These requirements would ensure that: (1) sellers of bulk power do not construct costly central station power plants to support transactions until all less expensive demand-side or generating measures are implemented; (2) conservation entrepreneurs can compete on equal terms with power suppliers for out-of-state markets; and (3) buyers do not substitute interstate purchases for less costly end-use or supply resources in their own system.

Our proposal does not apply to short-term power transfers, which account for the bulk of FERC-regulated commerce. However, there is increasing interest in power transfer arrangements covering three years or more, which are both more lucrative and more significant from environmental and resource planning perspectives. The approach recommended here is consistent with that already used by the Bonneville Power Administration in its long-term power marketing.[90] Moreover, our proposal will not interfere with efforts to increase access to the transmission grid for municipal utilities and power customers.

Proposal: Conduct research and evaluation to improve utility, state, and local energy conservation programs.

Utilities, states and localities are spending at least $1 billion per year on conservation and load management programs. Only limited research, however, has been conducted on alternative forms of program design and delivery. Considerable uncertainty remains about the significance of different program elements, response rates, and the net effects these programs have on energy demand and peak loads.[91]

DOE provides limited support for experimentation and evaluation related to state and utility conservation programs. But a much more intensive effort is called for to improve both the quality and understanding of conservation programs. Although not very costly, this effort is important and should not be overlooked by energy policymakers.

We propose that DOE establish and manage this program together with the Electric Power Research Institute, Gas Research Institute, utility commissions, and state energy agencies. The program should: (1) develop guidelines for conservation program experiments and evaluations, (2) provide technical assistance to utilities, states, and local agencies, and (3) conduct research and demonstrate new techniques for evaluating the impacts of conservation programs. As an added benefit, this program will improve the ability of states and utilities to conduct least-cost planning.

A number of states and utilities have proven that careful program evaluation and experimentation are well worth the effort. For example, Wisconsin used evaluations and experiments to greatly increase energy

41

savings and lower costs in its low-income weatherization program.[92] A well-funded and prominent national evaluation effort could provide similar benefits throughout the country.

Enhancing Industrial Competitiveness with Energy-Efficiency Research

American industry has faced few challenges as serious as today's international competition. Efficient foreign manufacturers have deeply penetrated American markets that were once the exclusive domain of domestic manufacturers. Since the early 1970s, the market shares of U.S. manufacturers have declined in a wide variety of product areas, including automobiles, steel, machine tools, telecommunications equipment, and semiconductors.[93] To meet the challenge, American industry must improve its efficiency as well as the value and quality of its products.

Energy costs American manufacturers over $100 billion each year. Despite impressive gains in the last decade, U.S. industry is far less energy efficient than most of its major trade competitors. (See Table 3.) Improving the energy efficiency of American industry, especially energy-intensive industries, can make U.S. industry more competitive by reducing the final cost of products. Innovative energy-efficient technologies such as thin strip steel casting (which eliminates a cool-down/reheat step in steel making), foam processing for textiles (which substitutes foam for water in textile processing and thus reduces energy needed to dry fabric),[94] and impulse paper drying (which mechanically forces moisture out of paper, leaving less moisture that must be evaporated with energy-intensive processes)[95] can greatly reduce production costs for industry.

Several studies suggest that successful innovations tend to offer benefits not just in energy use, but in labor, materials, capital, and product quality. The innovations listed above all provide multiple benefits.[96] Foam processing, for example, can greatly improve a textile mill's production rate. Thus, energy efficiency will be advanced by industrial process innovation aimed at solving many problems simultaneously.

Improving the efficiency of energy-consuming *products* sold by American industry is also an important means of making American industry

Table 3. Industrial Energy Intensity, Selected Countries

Country	Industrial energy use per unit of industrial value added (a) 1985	Average annual change during 1973–85 (b) (%)
West Germany	0.18	−3.0
Italy	0.23	−2.7
Japan	0.21	−4.7
Sweden	0.29	−1.9
United Kingdom	0.24	−3.0
United States	0.43	−2.4

(a) Expressed in tonnes of oil equivalent per 1000 1980 U.S. dollars.
(b) Based on each country's own currency.

SOURCE: Energy Conservation Indicators in IEA Countries, *International Energy Agency, OECD, Paris, 1987.*

more competitive. The vast array of industries that manufacture energy-consuming equipment, including the makers of residential appliances, commercial heating and cooling equipment, automobiles, and electric motors stand at the threshold of an enormous international market for advanced, energy-efficient products. Japanese and American researchers, for example, are engaged in a race to develop gas-fired residential heat pumps, which promise to be about twice as efficient as the best gas furnaces available today. And a few strong-selling new technologies such as low-emissivity windows (which use super thin, transparent metallic coatings to reduce heat radiated through windows) have demonstrated the market potential for energy-efficient products.

Unfortunately, U.S. industry significantly under-invests in technology development.[97] This under-investment stems from a number of factors, including the uncertainty that research will bear fruit, its long payback period, difficulties in capturing the benefits of research, and the expense of maintaining research programs during economic downturns. Fragmented industries are constrained in R&D spending because relatively small companies have little incentive to conduct research that benefits more than their small part of the market. And in mature industrial sectors, large firms often are not inclined to develop products or processes that make their investment in existing plant and equipment obsolete. Therefore, the private sector cannot be expected to conduct the full range of research the country needs.[98]

Just as important, U.S. industry often has difficulty commercializing new technologies it develops. Among the notable examples are video cassette recorders and industrial robots, both of which were developed by U.S. companies but commercialized primarily by Japanese companies. We propose the following policy measures to enhance the technological capabilities of industry and its ability to introduce new technologies in the market.

Proposal: Increase the commitment to federal energy-efficiency research and development and re-establish the federal role in demonstrating new energy-efficient technologies.

During the past seven years, the DOE conservation R&D budget has been slashed by more than 50 percent. This occurred despite its many successful R&D projects which will eventually yield billions of dollars of energy savings.[99] Textile foam processing, impulse paper drying, and low-emissivity windows all have been supported by this program. Andersen Windows, the largest U.S. window maker, estimates that low-emissivity windows now account for more than half of the company's window sales.[100] Electronic ballasts for fluorescent lamps, another technology advanced by the program, cut electricity use for fluorescent lighting by about 25 percent and are expected to save consumers about $2 billion per year by the mid-1990s. Many opportunities remain for similarly impressive advancements. The federal energy conservation R&D program should, therefore, be substantially expanded.

The federal government should also recommit to conducting low-cost demonstrations of new energy-efficient technologies. Such demonstrations will give scientists and engineers an opportunity to apply and prove innovative technology in the real world. Demonstrations are often necessary to encourage risk-averse companies to adopt new technologies. Small-scale demonstrations played an important role in establishing the market viability of many of DOE's successful conservation R&D projects.[101] Unlike most energy supply technology demonstrations (for example, synfuels and the liquid metal fast breeder reactor), conservation technologies have the advantage of being relatively inexpensive to demonstrate.

The proposed demonstrations should be conducted in close cooperation with industry, and industry should share substantially in the cost. This requirement should limit premature demonstrations. As technologies are advanced, and risks are reduced, the government's share of costs should decrease, or in some circumstances, be eliminated. The appropriate level of cost-sharing should be determined on a case-by-case basis and be influenced by such factors as the ability of the proposer to share the costs, the vested interest of the proposer, the residual rights required by the proposer, and the risk of project failure. The government should approach demonstrations cautiously.

Both the Gas Research Institute (GRI) and the Electric Power Research Institute (EPRI) recognize the importance of demonstrations in the innovation process. GRI, which spends about half of its $170 million budget on efficiency projects, has researched and demonstrated such important technologies as pulse combustion furnaces, advanced commerical cooking equipment, and industrial heat recovery devices.[102] EPRI supported research and demonstration of a highly innovative, efficient variable-speed heat pump, which Carrier Corporation plans to market soon.[103]

Demonstration programs, and the research that precedes them, should also be based on a long-term commitment of funding as long as technical milestones are met. Industry is generally reluctant to participate in research and demonstration without such commitments because federal programs are often scaled down or re-directed after they have begun. Some countries with which the United States competes have multi-year funding commitments for research. The Japanese government's energy conservation R&D program approves project funding levels for up to ten years. Hence, the U.S. government should explore alternatives to annual R&D appropriations with provision for oversight.

Energy Efficiency

Proposal: Establish research centers for energy-intensive industrial processes.

Energy-intensive industries can benefit the most from new, energy-efficient industrial processes. But like most American industries they under-invest in research. We therefore propose that the federal government establish research centers for energy-intensive industrial processes.

The proposed centers would conduct basic and applied research on common industrial processes, such as removing contaminants from post-consumer steel scrap and processing it into high-quality products; membrane separation processes; chemical processing in a molten metal bath; metal casting, forging, and powder forming; fuel refining; and paper making. Over 50 areas in manufacturing processes merit federal support in the form of basic technology centers.[104] The centers would not focus exclusively on energy-efficiency research. Rather, they would research these processes to develop multiple improvements, one of which would be energy efficiency.

The centers would serve initially as the catalyst and later as the core of a larger industry research effort. Assurances of a high degree of cooperation and coordination from industry would be sought before each center would be established. The centers could be organized as "national user facilities," in which government would provide research facilities that industry could use for conducting proprietary or public domain research. A strong technology transfer program would be an essential element in each center.

The research conducted by the National Advisory Committee for Aeronautics (NACA) after World War I is a good example of this kind of research effort. NACA did not design aircraft or its components, but it researched technologies that were fundamental to the aircraft industry, such as airfoil shapes. After being changed to NASA, it led in the development of noise-suppression techniques and turbofans for jet engines.[105]

The Combustion Research Program operated by Sandia National Laboratories is a paradigm of the proposed centers. This program fills a niche between universities and industry and is a catalyst for an aggressive, focused, national program. It conducts basic research on combustion phenomena and applied research on combustion processes occurring in internal combustion engines, furnaces, and coal combustors. The insight generated through its research is incorporated into computer models which can guide the development of more-efficient, fuel-flexible combustion hardware. Industry is deeply involved in research and management of the program. The center's core budget is provided by the government, but companies such as General Motors, Ford, and Cummins Diesel supplement those funds and conduct research of their own at the facility.

Results from the Combustion Research Program are being widely disseminated through a very active visiting scientist program, and more directly through industry involvement in research. The scientific results of the program are typically in the public domain, although proprietary work can also be conducted by firms using the facilities.

Selection of technologies for the proposed R&D centers should not be confined to applications of newly discovered scientific phenomena such as lasers, bioengineering, or superconductivity. Many older processes remain critical to the nation's industrial infrastructure and are ripe for technological innovation. In fact, new high technology capabilities have revolutionized research itself and have created opportunities for new understanding of phenomena incorporated in traditional industrial processes.

Many technologies, of course, have a clear high-technology focus. Some of these are being addressed in the Engineering Research Centers created by the National Science Foundation (NSF) and in the University Research Initiative of the Department of Defense. Care should be exercised not to overlap these efforts.

Creating technology research centers of high quality will require a gradual but ambitious process. It will also require careful selection of a lead agency (which could be the Department of Energy or the NSF) and cooperation among federal agencies. We envision a multi-year program, with each center assured of long-term support. The average federal contribution per center would be about $5-10 million dollars annually. Private industry would be expected to contribute heavily to the centers. We recommend that about ten such centers be established by the early 1990s. If early experience is positive, the program could be expanded.

Proposal: Establish a program to monitor and distribute information on foreign energy-efficiency research.

The United States has been the well-spring of new technologies for so long that it often ignores foreign technology research and innovation. Meanwhile, foreign countries have closely monitored new technology developments in the U.S. The rapid rise in technological capabilities of many foreign countries now makes it necessary for the U.S. to monitor more closely their new technology developments.

This initiative would establish a program to monitor and distribute information on foreign research and development activities for advanced energy-efficient technologies. It would complement the previous two proposals by providing current information on key foreign technical activities related to energy efficiency.

The program would evaluate foreign energy research, technology developments, and advanced system installations, and would assess the impact of foreign technology development on the United States, especially with regard to U.S. technical standing in world markets. This information would help identify the technological needs of domestic firms, guide federal research investments, and identify the export potential for energy-efficient products and process technologies produced in the United States. The research monitoring program would also maintain an information service capable of supporting foreign literature and patent searches and make industry aware of its services.

This effort would accelerate the development of conservation technology and would increase opportunities to apply advanced U.S. or foreign technology. Understanding foreign energy use and research activities would help the government to avoid "reinventing the wheel."

Making Buildings More Efficient to Improve Their Affordability

Each year the United States spends about $170 billion on energy for buildings, nearly half of the total annual U.S. energy bill. High energy costs are especially hard on the poor, who tend to live in old, poorly maintained, and inefficient buildings. Families below the poverty line spend an average 19 percent of their income on home energy costs, which is more than four times the percentage spent by middle-income families.[106] According to federal guidelines, a third of renters and almost half of low-income families are cost-burdened—that is, they pay an unacceptably high percentage of their income for housing.[107, 108] A recent analysis estimates that an across-the-board 25 percent reduction in residential energy use, an amount both technically and economically feasible, would make housing affordable for an additional 2 million households, more than half of which would be low-income households.[109]

The potential for improving the energy efficiency of U.S. buildings is large. If all cost-effective conservation measures were employed, energy consumed in buildings could be reduced by 30-50 percent.[110] But many obstacles impede further efficiency improvements. For example, split incentives between builders and building owners, and between landlords and tenants discourage conservation investments. Builders are more concerned with minimizing first costs than life-cycle costs, and landlords whose tenants pay their own energy bills have little incentive to make improvements.[111] Consumers also often lack the information and capital necessary to invest in efficiency improvements or to demand energy-efficient construction.

Many programs to help overcome these and other obstacles already exist. Utility conservation programs, such as rebates to consumers who purchase efficient appliances and lighting products are proliferating. New efforts to provide least-cost utility services will lead to improved building efficiency. But these efforts should be expanded, and new efforts are needed if the United States is to tap even part of the enormous conservation potential in buildings.

Indoor air quality, an important issue related to energy efficiency in buildings, also merits further attention. Any adverse effect that caulking and weatherstripping have on the concentration of indoor pollutants can be dealt with by addressing pollutants at their source. Researchers have found that indoor air pollution concentrations have a much stronger relationship with pollutant sources and source emission rates than with air infiltration rates.[112] Most tight, energy-efficient houses have acceptable air quality, while leaky homes are not immune to poor air quality. With home heating and cooling bills averaging about $500 per year, haphazard leakiness can be an expensive way to have, at best, limited control over indoor air pollution. Indoor pollutants are best controlled at their source.

The following recommended policy measures are insufficient to reap all of the potential for energy conservation benefits in the buildings sector, but they could make a major contribution. These recommendations support and complement the many successful efforts being made by state regulatory agencies, utilities, builders, and consumers.

Proposal: Improve the effectiveness of and increase funding for low-income weatherization, especially for multi-family buildings.

At the current rate of weatherization, at least 40 years will be needed to weatherize the existing stock of eligible low-income homes. Weatherization programs operated by the federal and state governments, utilities, and other organizations reach only a small percentage of the more than 17 million low-income homes that need to be weatherized.

We propose that federal, state and local governments, and utilities expand their commitment to improving the energy efficiency of low-income housing. The federal government should at least double its annual investment in low-income weatherization. Doubling is far less than can be justified, but it would be an important step toward relieving the enormous energy cost burden of low-income homes. Furthermore, state and local governments can encourage increased market demand for more efficient buildings by requiring home energy performance rating systems, which enable potential renters and buyers to estimate energy costs before choosing a house or apartment.

The need for weatherization is especially acute in multi-family buildings, which have a high concentration of low-income families and have undergone few efficiency improvements. To help, the federal government should increase funds available through the federal Solar Energy and Energy Conservation Bank, and earmark them for multi-family housing weatherization. The Bank has been a small but important source of funds for multi-family weatherization programs because it offers highly flexible funding that allows local organizations to design approaches that best suit local needs. Its funds have been used to leverage much larger private investment in multi-family buildings. Massachusetts, for instance, uses Bank funds to reduce the principal of private loans for conservation improvements to multi-family buildings. States wanting to participate in the multi-family program should commit matching funds. The combined federal and state funds would be used to improve the terms of private loans.

The loans could be channelled through existing and newly established non-profit energy service companies modeled after successful efforts such as the Citizens Conservation Corporation in Boston, the Center for Neighborhood Technology in Chicago, and the Energy Resource Center in Saint Paul, Minnesota. These organizations are suggested as models because they have been particularly effective at reducing energy use in multi-family buildings. The Citizens Conservation Corporation, for example, provides both technical and financial services to multi-family buildings through arrangements that use energy savings to service weatherization loans, and in some cases to reward tenants for conserving. The organization reports average energy savings in the 20-50 percent range.[113] Other types of organizations such as local housing agencies could also help administer the program.

But before greatly expanding funding for weatherization, the technical ability to weatherize buildings needs to be improved. Evaluations of the low-income weatherization program indicate that much room for technical improvement remains.[114] A recent research project in Wisconsin showed that using new technologies and a new procedure for choosing weatherization measures could produce twice the energy savings of the old Wisconsin Weatherization Program at about 25 percent less cost.[115] Another research project in Minnesota tested innovative weatherization procedures and found that dramatic improvements in the cost effectiveness of weatherization could be achieved.[116] Based on the success of these and other research efforts, we recommend that a weatherization research program be established in the U.S. Department of Energy, with a goal of increasing the energy savings to investment ratio of the low-income weatherization program by at least 50 percent.

Weatherization programs should also be modified to improve indoor air quality in low-income homes. National data indicate that at least 15 percent of all households have elevated levels of radon and other indoor air pollutants.[117] Weatherization organizations are in an ideal position to assess indoor air quality in low-income buildings. With adequate training, they could test for radon and combustion gases during weatherization visits. Measures to mitigate identified problems could be installed by weatherization crews or other contractors specializing in indoor air quality.

The seriousness of the low-income weatherization and housing affordability problem demands the nation's attention. Rather than continue with minimal weatherization funding, and little attention to improving its effectiveness, it is time to redouble our efforts to make housing more affordable for those most in need. Improving energy efficiency is key to that effort.

Proposal: Establish federal minimum efficiency standards for fluorescent and incandescent lamps.

Lighting accounts for one-fifth of all the electricity consumed in the U.S. Although high efficiency lamps and lighting equipment are very cost effective for consumers—with simple paybacks on the order of one to three years—consumers do not routinely purchase efficient lamps because they lack information, they fail to examine life-cycle cost, and because lighting equipment buyers frequently are not the people who pay for the energy this equipment consumes.[118]

Similar problems impede the purchase of more efficient consumer appliances. To address the problem, Congress adopted minimum efficiency standards in 1987 for refrigerators, water heaters, air conditioners, and other appliances. These standards are projected to reduce peak electricity demand in the year 2000 by 22,000 megawatts, equivalent to the output of about 22 large nuclear power plants.[119] Further upgrading these standards, as required by the law, could provide even greater savings.

We propose that Congress adopt similar national minimum efficiency standards for a number of common lamps. The standards for fluorescent lamps should be strong enough to ensure that only lamps as efficient as those that use improved phosphors could be produced. Standards for incandescent lamps should be set so that only those as efficient as krypton-filled lamps could be produced. Such standards would be highly cost-effective for consumers and could be met by many products already commercially available. The standards should be periodically reviewed by the Department of Energy and strengthened if justified.

The proposed lamp standards would complement efficiency standards for fluorescent lamp ballasts. California, Massachusetts, New York, and Florida have already enacted ballast efficiency standards. Congress recently passed a bill that set national minimum efficiency standards for ballasts.

The lamp standards we propose could by the year 2000 reduce electricity consumption by 25 billion kilowatt hours per year, save consumers about $1.9 billion per year, and reduce peak electric demand by 5,000 megawatts, equivalent to the peak demand of about two and a half million households.

Proposal: Improve the energy efficiency of federal buildings.

Federal buildings, excluding public housing, annually consume about $4 billion worth of energy. Largely because of limited resources and lack of government-wide support, the 12-year-old Federal Energy Management Program has had little effect on federal government energy consumption. In addition, efficiency improvements in federal buildings have been severely hampered by lack of incentives for federal facility managers to reduce energy costs, lack of capital to make improvements, and lack of model federal facilities to demonstrate the effectiveness of energy-efficiency measures.[120]

We propose a serious and comprehensive commitment to improve the energy efficiency of federal buildings. The effort should establish new incentives and guidelines for federal officials. Agency managers, for example, could be allowed to retain part of their energy savings to meet other budgetary needs of their agency. Guidelines for investment in conservation measures should unambiguously require minimum life-cycle costs. New aggressive energy conservation goals for federal buildings should be set, such as 25 percent savings per square foot of floor space within ten years. And model federal facilities can be used as showcases to bolster the overall effort.

The effort should also include technical and institutional research and information programs, taking advantage of the expertise residing in the national laboratories and other research centers. The program should also seek improvements for indoor air quality and thermal comfort.

Although the conservation potential in all government buildings has not been analyzed, the age of the buildings, the lack of incentives to make improvements, and the relatively low-level of conservation retrofit investment indicate that considerable energy saving potential exists. Reducing its energy bill could help the federal government reduce its budget deficit, and help establish the viability of new conservation technologies and procedures, which, in turn, could lead to improvements in the efficiency of private buildings.

The biggest challenge of this effort is to train and motivate federal facility managers to make energy-efficient, cost-effective improvements, show them how to finance these improvements, and help them institutionalize the process for making these improvements. Government employees responsible for implementing successful conservation projects should be recognized and financially rewarded.

Increased energy-efficiency efforts should also be directed at federally-assisted housing, which has a $2 billion annual energy bill. The responsible agency—the Department of Housing and Urban Development—has a dismal record in energy conservation. Evaluations of past energy retrofit performance and technical assistance for future retrofits are badly needed.

Proposal: Expand federal technical assistance for conservation efforts.

The experience of the last 15 years has shown that any effort to improve energy efficiency in buildings should be firmly based on strong technology development, program evaluation, and technical support.[121] New technologies are regularly expanding the bounds of energy saving potential. Program evaluation verifies whether anticipated energy savings are achieved and provide important feedback for making improvements. Technical support usually makes the difference between successful and unsuccessful conservation programs.

We suggest two particularly important technical support initiatives. A national technical assistance effort should be established to support utilities and local and state governments adopting building labeling and information programs. Building labeling rates the energy efficiency of buildings to enable prospective buyers and renters to make more informed decisions. Building efficiency labels are akin to the automobile fuel economy labels and appliance energy guide labels required by the federal government. The technical assistance program would provide: guidelines for program design, implementation, and evaluation; access to simple and accurate building design tools; evaluation reports on the experience of related programs; and direct consultation with program experts.

We also propose that the federal government provide technical and managerial support for state and local governments adopting energy-conserving building codes. Building energy codes are a convenient and effective mechanism for accomplishing large energy savings at low cost in new buildings because it is easier and less expensive to build energy efficiency into new buildings than modify existing ones. Building codes also offer one of the few institutional mechanisms that brings together all people involved in the construction of a building—owners, developers, builders, lenders, design teams, and government regulators.

Many state and local governments, however, experience difficulty in developing and enforcing advanced codes because of their technical complexity. The federal government, which gained substantial expertise by developing Federal Building Energy Performance Standards, could provide compliance methods, educational materials for builders and code officials, and other technical support. This low-cost effort could have a major impact on the energy efficiency of new buildings, as demonstrated by California's success with codes containing stringent energy-efficiency requirements.[122]

Helping Developing Nations Acquire Skills and Technology for Energy Efficiency

Energy poses serious problems for developing countries and, consequently, the world at large. In the early 1980s, many developing countries spent 20-60 percent of their export earnings on imported oil.[123] Many countries suffer from shortages of electricity or fuels; others find it difficult to obtain the financing for costly energy supply projects. Utility borrowing in many developing countries already accounts for over one-third of total foreign debt.[124] And fuelwood and crop residues—the traditional energy sources of the poor—grow increasingly scarce.[125]

Increasing energy efficiency can reduce the urgent energy problems in developing countries, stimulate their economic growth, raise living standards, and improve environmental conditions. Opportunities for cost-effective efficiency improvements abound.[126] In Brazil, for example, potential exists to cut electricity demand in 2000 by 20 percent at one-fifth the cost of new power supply facilities.[127] A recent U.S. Agency for International Development (AID) report indicated that through conservation, developing countries could avoid $1.4 trillion in power supply expansion costs by 2008.[128] For the majority of citizens in developing countries who still use biofuels for cooking, increasing efficiency or shifting to modern cooking fuels can greatly reduce energy use, fuel costs, and the long hours spent collecting fuel.[129]

Why should policymakers in the United States take an interest in the energy priorities of developing countries? First, increasing efficiency in developing countries will improve their economic productivity and free foreign exchange for essential imports and debt service. Second, rising oil demand in developing countries—which could account for over half of the additional demand for oil among all non-communist countries during 1985-2000–places upward pressure on world oil prices.[130] Third, the need for energy efficiency in developing countries has the potential to create a new export market for the United States. Finally, developing nations could be responsible for one-third of worldwide coal use and over one-quarter of total commercial energy use by 1995.[131] Thus, their energy efficiency will significantly affect the rate of global warming and other environmental problems.

But implementing greater efficiency on a large scale in developing countries requires involvement of governments, utilities, the private sector, and international lending and aid agencies. Unfortunately, energy efficiency receives very little support from the multilateral development banks, AID, and other organizations providing assistance to developing countries. The ongoing energy crisis in developing countries calls for a major reorientation. Bilateral and multilateral assistance agencies should make energy efficiency the centerpiece of their energy programs.

Priority Policies

Proposal: Modify the energy planning and lending policies of the World Bank and other multilateral lending and development institutions.

U.S. officials should attempt to reform the energy lending and assistance policies of the World Bank, the regional development banks, and relevant United Nations organizations. These institutions provide much of the funding and technical assistance for energy projects in developing countries. In some cases, these institutions strongly influence the energy policies of host countries. The United States is a major donor to these multilateral institutions and can advocate a fundamental reorientation in energy planning and lending.

We propose that U.S. representatives on the boards of the multilateral development banks advocate the following reforms.

- Apply integrated least-cost planning principles to energy planning and lending activities.
- Provide substantial financing for improving the efficiency of energy production and use where technically and economically feasible.
- Provide technical assistance for establishing and implementing conservation programs.
- Provide support for policies within developing countries that encourage conservation and efficiency improvements—pricing and taxation policies which reflect the real costs of energy, standards and labeling policies to help overcome market imperfections, for example.

The Foreign Assistance Appropriations Bill for 1989 passed by the House of Representatives proposes some measures along these lines.[132] To adopt these provisions as U.S. policy, Congress may have to amend the Foreign Assistance Act and the International Financial Institutions Act.

The first reform mentioned above institutionalizes comparison of end-use efficiency options with new energy supply options and establishes least-cost energy services as a primary objective for the multilateral organizations. Of course, other critical objectives such as job creation, infrastructure building, and self-reliance need to be considered as well when setting energy priorities. Likewise, energy costs should be considered when evaluating a wide range of development options—expansion of energy-intensive industries or transportation systems, for example.

The second and third reforms ensure that developing countries receive the funds and technical assistance necessary to implement greater efficiency on a broad scale. Besides funding investments in energy efficiency, it will be necessary to establish efficiency research, financing, incentives, standards, education, and monitoring programs within developing countries. These are unfamiliar areas to developing countries and assistance agencies alike. Moreover, due to the diffuse nature of efficiency implementation, new mechanisms for accomplishing these tasks—for example, ways to disperse funds and manage programs for greater energy efficiency—must be developed. Consequently, technical and policy support, institution building, and program experimentation will be critical.

The fourth reform concerns policies within developing countries, such as energy pricing, equipment duties, sales taxes, product standards, and building codes. While not solely pertaining to energy efficiency, all can strongly influence levels of conservation and efficiency improvement.

A few precedents exist for these initiatives. The United States often applies leverage to alter the policies of the multilateral development banks.[133] In the past, the World Bank has supported industrial energy conservation and fuel substitution programs in a number of developing countries.[134] The World Bank also helped to establish a national electricity conservation program in Brazil.[135] Despite these precedents, conservation still receives minimal funding and attention from the World Bank and the regional development banks.

Proposal: Provide technology and policy assistance for energy efficiency to developing countries through U.S. AID and other American agencies.

We propose that AID and other U.S. government organizations, such as the Trade and Development Program and the Export-Import Bank, expand their efforts to help developing nations acquire technologies, policies, and programs for greater energy efficiency. But rather than take a traditional project orientation, this initiative would focus on building the capabilities of individuals and institutions within developing nations in both their governmental and non-governmental organizations.

This effort would draw heavily on the wealth of conservation expertise in the United States among utilities, state and local agencies, the private sector, non-governmental organizations, universities, and national laboratories. U.S. experts would be made available to their counterparts in developing countries. These individuals could help to strengthen local capability while assisting in activities such as development of least-cost energy plans, adapting conservation technologies to local conditions as well as new technology development, and organizing conservation programs. Similarly, appropriate institutions in the United States should be encouraged and funded to host and train professionals from developing countries.

U.S. AID should set an example for other assistance organizations, both within the United States and from other countries, by adopting a least-cost energy services approach and involving representatives from developing countries in setting energy assistance priorities. In addition, AID should support related activities such as R&D on efficient fossil fuel or biofuel-based technologies, technical and program data bases, and information exchange among developing countries.

Increasing private sector involvement in energy efficiency in developing countries is also needed. Organizations such as the Overseas Private Investment Corporation, the Export-Import Bank, and the Trade and Development Program should actively encourage U.S. companies to market and establish joint ventures in energy-efficient technologies and services in developing countries. Also, these agencies and AID should support, in part, the development and adaptation of American technologies to local conditions.

Energy conservation assistance and capability building is already supported to a limited degree by AID. For example, Lawrence Berkeley Laboratory is assisting Southeast Asian nations with the evaluation of conservation potential in commercial buildings and establishment of building codes. Technology R&D and market studies related to more efficient use of biomass residues are underway. And a new AID project supports research and development of technologies for the efficient supply and end use of energy in India.[136]

But AID and the other governmental organizations have not made the strong, long-term commitment to "person-to-person" exchange and institution building that is proposed here. We suggest funding on the order of $50-100 million per year for a number of years in order to make a significant contribution towards establishing energy conservation capability and efforts in developing countries. This is a modest proposal considering that the United States spends about $12 billion per year for non-military assistance to developing countries—but it could provide multiple benefits that serve the vital interests of the U.S.

Conclusion

No doubt policymakers will want to know what will be accomplished if the measures recommended here are implemented. How much energy savings will result and how much money will consumers save? How much will it cost or save the federal government? And how will our national security, industrial competitiveness, and environment be affected?

It is difficult to answer these questions. The impacts from some proposals—such as vehicle and lighting efficiency standards—can be calculated. But the impacts of many of the other proposals such as expanded R&D efforts and incentives for promoting least-cost utility services are highly uncertain.

Rather than attempting to quantify the energy savings of these specific policy proposals, we have estimated what might occur if the national goal of reducing energy intensity by 2.5 percent per year is realized. In this section, we present three scenarios for energy use in the United States at the turn of the century—the current Department of Energy forecast, a moderate efficiency case, and a high efficiency case.

Both the moderate and high efficiency scenarios are derived from other recent studies that consider what might occur given varying degrees of emphasis on energy efficiency.[137] The moderate efficiency scenario is based on existing policies and market trends, while the high efficiency scenario assumes expanded policy initiatives in support of conservation and widespread adoption of cost-effective efficiency measures. In short, the high efficiency scenario is consistent with adoption of our policy agenda.

The moderate efficiency scenario shows energy use increasing to 81

61

Table 4. Scenarios for U.S. Energy Use in 2000

| | Energy Use (Quads) | | | |
Sector	Actual 1987 (a)	High efficiency 2000 (b)	Moderate efficiency 2000 (b)	EIA base case 2000 (c)
Residential	15.7	15.6	17.3	18.3
Commercial	11.9	13.3	14.7	15.1
Industrial	27.2	23.8	28.0	33.8
Transportation	21.2	18.5	21.0	22.3
Total	76.0	71.2	81.0	89.6

Notes:
(a) "Monthly Energy Review," DOE/EIA-0035(87/12), Energy Information Administration, Washington, DC, Dec. 1987. This source combines residential and commercial energy use; the division shown above is based on the 1985 breakdown.
(b) Based on Reference 137.
(c) "Annual Energy Outlook 1987," DOE/EIA-0383(87), Energy Information Administration, Washington, DC, March 1988.

SOURCE: *American Council for an Energy-Efficient Economy.*

Quads by 2000. (See Table 4.) This outcome is still nearly 10 percent less than the most recent "base case" forecast by the Energy Information Administration (EIA) of the Department of Energy.[138] In all cases, GNP is assumed to grow at an annual rate of 2.0 to 2.5 percent. Consequently, the moderate efficiency scenario represents about a 1.7 percent annual rate of decrease in energy intensity between 1987-2000.

Our high efficiency scenario shows the United States consuming 71.2 Quads in 2000, 12 percent less than the moderate efficiency scenario and 21 percent less than the 89.6 Quads forecast by the EIA. The average rate of reduction in U.S. energy intensity during 1987-2000 is about 2.7 percent per year in the high efficiency scenario. The United States

Conclusion

actually achieved this rate of energy intensity reduction between 1976 and 1986.

The appendix to this report estimates the impact on the federal budget of our policy proposals. By implementing the measures we recommend, the U.S. government would receive far more revenue (primarily through the vehicle fuels tax) than it would spend. The net revenue gain of our policy agenda could reach about $30 billion by 1992.

Following the high efficiency path would enhance our economic well-being, competitiveness, national security, and environment. Specific benefits that would accrue from lowering energy use at the turn of the century by 10-18 Quads follow.

- The United States would save $1.3-2.2 trillion over the next 20 years (1987 dollars). The total investment in conservation measures required to achieve this savings would be on the order of $300-500 billion.

- The nation would reduce the projected increase in oil imports by 2.0-3.6 million barrels per day. This would cut the U.S. oil import bill by $18-40 billion, and significantly reduce the likelihood of OPEC regaining control of the world oil market, hiking oil prices, and possibly threatening the flow of oil to the United States and its allies.

- U.S. industries would improve their competitiveness through lower energy costs. Deferring the need for investment in new power plants alone could free more than $100 billion for capital investment in other U.S. industries.

- The poor would benefit from lower energy costs, additional jobs, and more affordable housing.

- Americans would reduce environmental damage and the need for costly pollution control measures. For example, carbon dioxide emissions would be 12-20 percent lower in 2000 in the high efficiency scenario compared to the moderate efficiency scenario or EIA's forecast.

- Last but perhaps most important, the United States would do its part in a worldwide energy-efficiency campaign. Such a campaign will be especially important to the three-quarters of the world's people who live in less-developed countries.

The United States possesses the technical ingenuity and institutions necessary to create an energy-efficient economy. But doing so requires political determination. Energy-efficiency improvements will continue to slow in the absence of new leadership and coordinated national policy. By placing energy efficiency at the top of his agenda, the next President can help create a prosperous, secure, and environmentally sound nation.

Appendix

*T*able A-1 presents estimates of the direct costs and revenues to the federal government for implementing the energy-efficiency policy agenda. The costs and revenues do not consider indirect impacts due to changes in tax revenue or interest rates, for example. For many policy proposals, the budgetary impact will depend to a large degree on the specific details of the policies. The values in Table A-1 should be viewed as approximations.

Table A-1 shows that by implementing the proposed policies, the federal government could receive far more in new revenue than is required as federal expenditures. The gasoline and diesel fuels tax alone would provide about $30 billion by the third year of the program, even with part of the tax revenue rebated to low-income persons. Thus, pursuing energy efficiency can help the U.S. government to balance its budget, besides providing many other benefits.

Table A-1. Impact of the Policy Proposals on the Federal Budget
(million dollars)

REVENUES Policy proposal (a)	1990	1991	*fiscal year* 1992	1993	1994
Vehicle fuels tax (b)	6,100	18,400	30,600	36,700	36,700
Gas guzzler tax	220	340	500	800	1,100
TOTAL	6,320	18,740	31,100	37,500	37,800

EXPENDITURES Policy proposal (a)	1990	1991	*fiscal year* 1992	1993	1994
International energy efficiency protocol	2	5	10	10	10
International efficiency cooperation	5	10	15	15	15
Research to lower energy use and protect the ozone layer	5	10	15	15	15
Integrated energy and environmental planning	2	5	5	5	5
Gas sipper rebates	–	–	–	–	1,000
Utility incentives	1	1	2	2	2
Competitive bidding	1	1	2	2	2
Research and evaluation of utility conservation programs	5	10	10	10	10
Federal research, development and demonstration	250	300	300	400	400
Industrial research centers	20	40	60	80	100
International R&D monitoring	2	2	2	2	2
Low-income weatherization	200	240	280	320	350
Energy efficiency in federal buildings (net of energy savings)	260	380	570	710	730
Technical assistance for energy-efficient buildings	1	1	2	2	2
Energy efficiency assistance for developing countries	20	50	100	100	100
TOTAL	770	1,060	1,370	1,670	2,740

(a) Policy proposals without budget impacts are not included.

(b) Net revenue taking into account rebates to low-income persons, assuming the tax is limited to 30 cents per gallon. Greater revenue would be collected in 1992 and 1993 if the tax increases to 50 cents per gallon.

SOURCE: *American Council for an Energy-Efficient Economy*

References and Notes

1. V. Ramanthan, "The Greenhouse Theory of Climate Change: A Test by an Inadvertent Global Experiment," *Science*, April 15, 1988.

2. National Research Council, *Changing Climate: Report of the Carbon Dioxide Assessment Committee* (Washington: National Academy Press, 1983).

3. J.R. Trabalka, ed., *Atmospheric Carbon Dioxide and the Global Carbon Cycle* (Springfield, VA: National Technical Information Service, 1985).

4. I.M. Mintzer, *A Matter of Degrees: The Potential for Controlling the Greenhouse Effect* (Washington, D.C.: World Resources Institute, April 1987); W.U. Chandler, *Energy Productivity: Key to Environmental Protection and Economic Progress* (Washington, D.C.: Worldwatch Institute, 1985).

5. Adopting economically justifiable efficiency improvements between now and the year 2025 would reduce global sulfur emissions from 265 million tons per year to 135 million tons. Current sulfur emissions, by comparison, total 100 million tons worldwide. Chandler, *Energy Productivity: Key to Environmental Protection and Economic Progress.*

6. U.S. estimate as cited in H.S. Geller, M.R. Ledbetter, E.L. Miller, and P.M. Miller, *Acid Rain and Electricity Conservation*, American Council for an Energy-Efficient Economy and the Energy Conservation Coalition, Washington, D.C., June 1987. West German estimate from International Cooperative Programme Assessment and Monitoring of Air Pollution Effects on Forests, "Forest Damage and Air Pollution: Report on the 1986 Forest Damage Survey in Europe," Global Environmental Monitoring System, U.N. Environment Program, Nairobi, mimeographed, 1987.

7. International Energy Agency, *Energy Conservation in IEA Countries* (Paris: Organization for Economic Cooperation and Development, 1987).

8. Office of Technology Assessment, U.S. Congress, *Industrial Energy Use* (Washington, D.C.: U.S. Government Printing Office, 1983).

9. C.A. Berg, "Energy Conservation in Industry: The Present Approach, The Future Opportunities," Report to the President's Council on Environmental Quality, Washington, D.C., 1979.

10. J. Goldemberg, T.B. Johansson, A.K.N. Reddy, and R.H. Williams, *Energy for a Sustainable World* (Washington, D.C.: World Resources Institute, September 1987).

11. U.S. Department of Energy, *Energy Security: A Report to the President of the United States*, DOE/S-0057, Washington, D.C., March 1987.

12. U.S. Department of Energy, "Patterns of U.S. Energy Demand," DOE/PE-0076, Washington, D.C., August 1987.

13. Energy Information Administration, *Annual Energy Review 1986* (Washington, D.C.: U.S. Government Printing Office, 1986).

14. International Energy Agency, *Energy Conservation in IEA Countries.*

15. H.S. Geller, "Residential Equipment Efficiency: A State-of-the-Art Review," American Council for an Energy-Efficient Economy, Washington, D.C., 1988; H.S. Geller, "Commercial Building Equipment Efficiency: A State-of-the-Art Review," American Council for an Energy-Efficient Economy, Washington, D.C., 1988.

16. Energy Information Administration, *Monthly Energy Review December 1987*, U.S. Department of Energy, Washington, D.C., March 1988.

17. IEA, *Energy Conservation in IEA Countries.*

18. M.C. Holcomb, S.D. Floyd, S.L. Cagle, "Transportation Energy Data Book," Oak Ridge National Laboratory, Edition 9, April 1987.

19. Energy Information Administration, *Monthly Energy Review*, September 1987.

20. Energy Information Administration, *Annual Energy Outlook 1987*, DOE/EIA-0383(87), U.S. Department of Energy, Washington, D.C., March 1988.

21. R.H. Williams, "A Low Energy Future for the United States," *Energy*, Vol. 12, No. 10/11, pp. 929-944, 1987.

22. Goldemberg, Johansson, Reddy, and Williams, *Energy for a Sustainable World.*

23. E. Hirst, et al., "Improving Energy Efficiency: The Effectiveness of Government Action," *Energy Policy*, June 1982; J. Clinton, H. Geller, E. Hirst, "Review of Government and Utility Energy Conservation Programs," *Annual Review of Energy* (Palo Alto, CA: Annual Reviews, Inc., 1986).

24. H.S. Geller, "Residential Equipment Efficiency: A State-of-the-Art Review."

25. J. Clinton, H. Geller, E. Hirst, "Review of Government and Utility Energy Conservation Programs."

26. H. Geller, J.P. Harris, M.D. Levine, and A.H. Rosenfeld, "The Role of Federal Research and Development in Advancing Energy Efficiency: A $50 Billion Contribution to the U.S. Economy," *Annual Review of Energy* (Palo Alto, CA: Annual Reviews, Inc., 1987).

27. D. Cogan and S. Williams, *Generating Energy Alternatives: Demand-Side Management and Renewable Energy at America's Electric Utilities* (Washington, D.C.: Investor Responsibility Research Center, 1987).

References and Notes

28. J. Jaeger, W.C. Clark, J. Goodman, M. Oppenheimer, and G.M. Woodwell, "Developing Policies for Responding to Climatic Change," Summary Paper, Workshop on Developing Policies for Responding to Climatic Change, Villach, Austria (September 28-October 2, 1987), February 1988.

29. M.C. MacCracken and F.M. Luther, eds., *The Potential Climatic Impacts of Increasing Carbon Dioxide* (Springfield, VA: National Technical Information Service, December 1985); J.H. Gibbons and W.U. Chandler, *Energy: The Conservation Revolution* (New York: Plenum Press, 1981).

30. W.U. Chandler, "Carbon Dioxide Control Policies: The Case of China," *Climatic Change*, forthcoming.

31. For a recent review of the physical science of climatic change, see Ramanathan, "The Greenhouse Theory of Climate Change: A Test by an Inadvertent Global Experiment."

32. For excellent introductions to the subject, see S.H. Schneider and R.Londer, *The Coevolution of Climate and Life* (San Francisco: Sierra Club Books, 1984); H. Flohn, "Life on a Warmer Earth: Possible Climatic Consequences of Man-Made Global Warming," International Institute for Applied Systems Analysis, Laxenburg, Austria, 1981. For a recent discussion of forest impacts, see M.B. Davis, "Lags in Vegetation Response to Climatic Changes," Background Paper No. 5, Workshop on Developing Policies for Responding to Climatic Change, September 28-October 22, 1987.

33. I.M. Mintzer, *A Matter of Degrees: The Potential for Controlling the Greenhouse Effect.*

34. D. Hafemeister, H. Kelly, and B. Levi, eds., *Energy Sources: Conservation and Renewables* (New York: American Institute of Physics, 1985).

35. IEA, *Energy Conservation in IEA Countries.* Also, World Resources Institute and the International Institute for Environment and Development, *World Resources 1987* (New York: Basic Books, 1987).

36. Goldemberg, Johannson, Reddy, and Williams, *Energy for a Sustainable World*; W.U. Chandler, *Energy Productivity: Key to Environmental Protection and Economic Progress.*

37. International Energy Agency, *Energy Conservation in IEA Countries.*

38. Institute for Energy Economics, "China's Energy Situation, Present and Future," *NIRA Report*, Vol. 4, No. 1, 1987; Xu Shoubo, Presentation at the Workshop on Developing Country Energy Strategies: Implications for the Greenhouse Problem, U.S. Environmental Protection Agency and World Resources Institute, Washington, D.C., April 28-29, 1988.

39. I. Mintzer, "A Matter of Degrees: Energy Policy and the Greenhouse Effect," *Environmental Policy and Law*, Vol. 17, No. 6, December 1987. Also, R. Bierbaum, N. Sundt, and R. Friedman, "An Analysis of the Montreal Protocol," Staff paper, Office of Technology Assessment, U.S. Congress, Washington, D.C., December 1987.

Energy Efficiency

40. J. Edmonds, et al., *An Analysis of Possible Future Retention of Fossil Fuel CO_2* (Washington, D.C.: U.S. Department of Energy, September 1984).

41. Chandler, *Energy Productivity*. Also, see Mintzer, *A Matter of Degrees*.

42. Chandler, "Carbon Dioxide Control Policies."

43. P.J. Crutzen and M.O. Andreae, "Atmospheric Chemistry," in T.F. Malone and J.G. Roederer, eds., *Global Change* (Cambridge: Cambridge University Press, 1985); R.T. Watson, M.A. Geller, R.S. Stolarski, and R.F. Hampson, "Present State of Knowledge of the Upper Atmosphere," National Aeronautics and Space Administration, January 1986.

44. T.G. Statt, U.S. Dept. of Energy, "The Use of Chlorofluorocarbons in Refrigeration, Insulation and Mobile Air Conditioning in the United States," paper prepared for the EPA Conference on Substitutes and Alternatives to CFCs and Halons, Washington, D.C., Jan. 1988.

45. S.K. Fischer, F.A. Creswick, and J. Dieckmann, "Energy-Use Impact of Chlorofluorocarbon Restrictions in Refrigeration and Buildings Applications," draft, Oak Ridge National Laboratory, Oak Ridge, TN, November 1987.

46. D.B. Goldstein, P.M. Miller, and R.K. Watson, "Developing Cost Curves for Conserved Energy in New Refrigerators and Freezers: Demonstration of Methodology and Detailed Engineering Results," American Council for an Energy-Efficient Economy and Natural Resources Defense Council, Washington, D.C., January 1987.

47. U.S. Congress, Office of Technology Assessment, *Acid Rain and Transported Air Pollutants* (Washington, D.C.: U.S. Government Printing Office, June 1984).

48. Geller, et al., *Acid Rain and Electricity Conservation*. Also, R.H. Williams, "Using Acid Rain Controls to Promote U.S. Competitiveness and Innovation in the Electric Utility Industry," draft report, Center for Energy and Environmental Studies, Princeton University, Princeton, N.J., April 1988.

49. Geller, et al., *Acid Rain and Electricity Conservation*.

50. "Countdown Acid Rain: Ontario's Acid Gas Control Program for 1986-1994," Ministry of the Environment, Ontario, Canada, undated.

51. Geller et al., *Acid Rain and Electricity Conservation*.

52. "Conservation Report," California Energy Commission, Sacramento, CA, October 1986.

53. U.S. Congress, Office of Technology Assessment, *U.S. Oil Production: The Effect of Low Oil Prices* (Washington, D.C.: U.S. Government Printing Office, September 1987).

54. U.S. Department of Energy, "Patterns of U.S. Energy Demand," Washington, D.C., August 1987.

55. M. Holcomb, S. Floyd, and S. Cagle, *Transportation Energy Data Book: Edition 9.*

References and Notes

56. See, generally, Office of Technology Assessment, *Increased Automobile Fuel Efficiency and Synthetic Fuels* (Washington, D.C.: U.S. Government Printing Office, 1982), and C. Gray, Jr. and F. von Hippel, "The Fuel Economy of Light Vehicles," *Scientific American*, May 1981.

57. R.H. Williams, Princeton University, testimony before the Subcommittee on Energy Conservation and Power, Committee on Energy and Commerce, U.S. House of Representatives, July, 1983.

58. See D.L. Bleviss, *The New Oil Crisis and Fuel Economy Technologies: Preparing the Light Transportation Industry for the 1990s* (forthcoming from Greenwood Press, 1988).

59. OTA, *Increased Automobile Fuel Efficiency and Synthetic Fuels.*

60. OTA, *Increased Automobile Fuel Efficiency and Synthetic Fuels*; Energy and Environmental Analysis, *Analysis of the Capabilities of Domestic Auto Manufacturers to Improve CAFE*, 1986.

61. Bleviss, *The New Oil Crisis and Fuel Economy Technologies.*

62. H.G. Broadman, "Review and Analysis of Oil Import Premium Estimates," Discussion Paper D-82C, Energy and National Security Series, Resources for the Future, Washington, D.C., 1981; H.G. Broadman and W.W. Hogan, "Oil Tariff Policy in an Uncertain Market," Energy and Environmental Policy Center, Harvard University, 1986.

63. U.S. Department of Energy, *International Energy Annual 1986* (Washington, D.C.: 1987).

64. See R.H. Williams, "A $2 A Gallon Political Opportunity," and W.U. Chandler and H.L. Gwin, "Gasoline Conservation in an Era of Confrontation," in D. Yergin, ed., *The Dependence Dilemma: Gasoline Consumption and America's Security* (Cambridge, MA: Harvard University Center for International Affairs, 1980).

65. Analysis suggests that a large import fee—$10 per barrel or more—is justified on the basis of reduced macroeconomic losses and reduced risk of oil import disruption. Both the lower volume of purchases and the expected reduction in the world price contribute to the reduction in total cost to the United States, but at the expense of oil exporters. Another major benefit comes from reducing the risk of an oil crisis. That is, because the risk of a new spiral of oil price hikes as a result of oil shortages is high, the U.S. economy will benefit from the reduced upward pressure on prices that the oil tariff would provide.

    Unfortunately, an oil import fee would be difficult to implement. The free trade agreement between the United States and Canada would provide one large loophole. And the fee could create serious problems for the economies of important U.S. allies, including Mexico, Venezuela, and Saudi Arabia. Special exemptions or direct transfers of funds would be required, possibly making the import fee unworkable. The oil import fee, however, might appear acceptable as a second-best strategy.

66. J.H. Gibbons, et al., *Alternative Energy Demand Futures to 2010* (Washington, D.C.: National Academy of Sciences, 1979); F. von Hippel and B. Levi, "Automo-

bile Fuel Efficiency: The Opportunity and the Weakness of Existing Market Incentives," *Resources and Conservation*, Vol. 10, 1983.

67. B. McNutt and P. Patterson, "Cafe Standards—Is a Change in Form Needed?" SAE Technical Paper Series, 861424, 1986.

68. R.W. Crandall and J.D. Graham, "The Effect of Fuel Economy Standards on Automobile Safety," forthcoming in *The Journal of Law and Economics*.

69. Center for Auto Safety, "Higher Fuel Economy Does Not Lower Auto Safety," Washington, D.C., 1988.

70. Ibid.

71. Energy Information Administration, "Annual Energy Outlook 1987."

72. U.S. Department of Energy, "Patterns of U.S. Energy Demand."

73. "36th Annual Electric Utility Industry Forecast," *Electrical World*, September 1985.

74. R.C. Cavanagh, "Least-Cost Planning Imperatives for Electric Utilities and Their Regulators," *The Harvard Environmental Law Review* 10 (2), 1986. Also, "Least-Cost Electrical Strategies: An Information Packet," Energy Conservation Coalition, Washington, D.C., Jan. 1987.

75. Northwest Conservation and Electric Power Plan, Northwest Power Planning Council, Portland, OR, 1986.

76. P. Markowitz and J. Kriesberg, "Least-Cost Electrical Planning: Is There Really a State Movement?" Critical Mass Energy Project, Washington, D.C., December 1985. L. Shapiro, P. Markowitz, and N. Hirsh, "A Brighter Future: State Actions in Least-Cost Electrical Planning," Energy Conservation Coalition, Washington, D.C., Dec. 1987.

77. E. Berman, M. Cooper, and H. Geller, "A Compendium of Utility-Sponsored Energy Efficiency Rebate Programs," EPRI EM-5579, Electric Power Research Institute, Palo Alto, CA, 1987.

78. Cogan and Williams, *Generating Energy Alternatives*.

79. U.S. Department of Energy, *Energy Security*. Also, "The Adequacy of U.S. Electricity Supply Through the Year 2000," Utility Data Institute, Washington, D.C., March 1987.

80. California Public Utility Commission, Decision No. 91107, San Francisco, CA, 1979.

81. Massachusetts Department of Public Utilities, Order No. 85-266-A and 85-271-A, Boston, MA, June 26, 1986.

82. Interview with Douglas C. Bauer, *Electric Potential*, Vol. 3, No. 5, S.A. Mitnick and Associates, Arlington, VA, November-December 1987.

83. Wisconsin Public Service Commission, Opinion and Order 6630-UR-100, Madison, WI, Dec. 30, 1986.

References and Notes

84. R. Cavanagh, "Responsible Power Marketing in an Increasingly Competitive Era," *Yale Journal on Regulation*, Vol. 5, 1988 (forthcoming).

85. H.S. Geller, "Use of Financial Incentives to Encourage Least-Cost Utility Planning and Energy Efficiency," paper presented at the NARUC Least-Cost Planning Conference, Aspen, CO, April 1988. Also, D. Moskovitz, "Will Least-Cost Planning Work Without Significant Regulation Reform?" paper presented at the NARUC Least-Cost Planning Conference, Aspen, CO, April 1988.

86. R. Cavanagh, "The Role of Conservation Resources in Competitive Bidding Systems for Electricity Supply," Testimony before the Subcommittee on Energy and Power, Committee on Energy and Commerce, U.S. House of Representatives, Washington, D.C., March 31, 1988.

87. Personal communication with Mr. Douglas Herling, Central Maine Power Co., Augusta, ME, March 1988.

88. Researchers at Lawrence Berkeley and Oak Ridge National Laboratories will begin studying issues related to demand-side bidding in 1988. Personal communication with Mr. Joe Eto, Lawrence Berkeley Laboratory, Berkeley, CA, March 1988.

89. For example, see "Monongahela Power Company, et al., " Docket No. ER87-330-000, 39 FERC 61,350, 1987.

90. "Environmental Assessment: Proposed Contract with Southern California Edison," DOE/EA-0305, Bonneville Power Administration, Portland, OR, May 1986.

91 Clinton, Geller, and Hirst, "Review of Government and Utility Energy Conservation Programs."

92. C. Ghandehari, et al., "Low-Income Weatherization Study," four volumes, Department of Administration, Division of State Energy, Madison, WI, 1984. Also, M. Ternes, et al., "Field Test Evaluation of Conservation Retrofits of Low-Income Single Family Buildings in Wisconsin: A Summary Report," ORNL/CON-229, Oak Ridge National Laboratory, Oak Ridge, TN, 1988.

93. Office of Technology Assessment, U.S. Congress, *Paying the Bill: Manufacturing And America's Trade Deficit* (Washington, D.C.: U.S. Government Printing Office, July 1988).

94. U.S. Department of Energy, Industrial Energy Conservation Program, *Project Description Sheets*, Washington, D.C.

95. H.P. Lavery, "Impulse Paper Drying: An Overview," Institute of Paper Chemistry, Appleton, WI, 1988.

96. Berg, "Energy Conservation in Industry: the Present Approach, the Future Opportunities."

97. J.A. Young, *Global Competition—The New Reality: Results of the President's Commission on Industrial Competitiveness; The Positive Sum Strategy*, Landau R. and Rosenberg, N., eds., 1986 National Academy Press, Washington, D.C. Also, Office of Technology Assessment, "Paying the Bill: Manufacturing and America's Trade Deficit."

98. H. Brooks, "National Science Policy and Technological Innovation," in *The Positive Sum Strategy*, R. Landau and N. Rosenberg, eds., (Washington, D.C.: National Academy Press, 1986).

99. H.S. Geller, et al., "The Role of Federal Research and Development in Advancing Energy Efficiency: A $50 Billion Dollar Contribution to the U.S. Economy."

100. Andersen Corporation, News Release, Bayport, MN, January 5, 1988.

101. U.S. Department of Energy, Office of Conservation, *Energy Conservation Program Success Stories* (Washington, D.C.: U.S. Department of Energy, May 1987).

102. Gas Research Institute, 1986 and 1987 Annual Reports, Chicago, IL.

103. "All the Comforts of Home . . . and Then Some," *EPRI Journal*, Electric Power Research Institute, Palo Alto, CA, March 1988.

104. National Science Foundation, "Engineering, Program Activity Summary," FY 1986 estimated, and "FY 1988 budget to the Congress, Engineering," Washington, D.C.

105. Brooks, "National Science Policy and Technological Innovation."

106. W. Prindle and M. Reid, "Energy Efficiency: A Key to Affordable Housing," Alliance to Save Energy, Washington, D.C., January, 1988.

107. Federal guidelines define homeowners and renters as cost-burdened if their housing costs exceed 40 percent and 30 percent of income, respectively.

108. Prindle and Reid, "Energy Efficiency: A Key to Affordable Housing."

109. Ibid.

110. For example, the National Audubon Society's proposed National Energy Plan estimated that we could reduce energy use in buildings by 30% and save consumers $93 billion (1983 dollars) in the year 2000 with an annualized capital investment of only half ($47 billion) that amount. See, National Audubon Society, 1984, *The Audubon Energy Plan 1984*, National Audubon Society, New York. Another recent assessment concluded that U.S. residential and commercial energy demand could be reduced by 50% by the year 2020 if cost-effective efficiency improvements are implemented to the maximum extent. See, R.H. Williams, "A Low Energy Future for the United States."

111. D. Bleviss and A. Gravitz, *Energy Conservation and Rental Housing*, (Washington, D.C.: Energy Conservation Coalition, October 1984).

112. D.T. Grimsrud, et al., "A Comparison of Indoor Air Quality in Pacific Northwest Existing and New Energy-Efficient Homes," Lawrence Berkeley Laboratory, Berkeley, CA, 1986.

113. Bleviss and Gravitz, *Energy Conservation and Rental Housing.*

114. See, for example, Wisconsin Energy Conservation Corporation, *Low-Income Weatherization Program Study*, Madison, WI, Oct. 1984.

115. M. Ternes, et al., "Field Test Evaluation of Conservation Retrofits of Low-Income Single Family Buildings in Wisconsin."

References and Notes

116. M. Quaid and R. Faber, "Preliminary Evaluation of Coordinated Energy Savings," Minneapolis Energy Office, June 1988.

117. U.S. General Accounting Office, "Indoor Radon: Limited Federal Response to Reduce Contamination in Housing," GAO/RCED-88-103, Washington, D.C., April 1988.

118. Geller, "Commercial Building Equipment Efficiency: A State-of-the-Art Review."

119. H.S. Geller, "Energy and Economic Savings from National Appliance Efficiency Standards," American Council for an Energy-Efficient Economy, Washington, D.C., March, 1986.

120. Personal communications with Mr. Richard Brancato, Manager, Federal Energy Management Program, Department of Energy, Washington, D.C., February, 1988.

121. E. Hirst, et al., *Energy Efficiency in Buildings: Progress and Promise* (Washington, D.C.: American Council for an Energy-Efficient Economy, 1986).

122. J.A. Wilson, "Efficiency Standards in California's Energy Policy," *State Energy Policy*, S.W. Sawyer, J.R. Armstrong, eds. (Boulder, CO: Westview Press, 1985).

123. The World Bank, *World Development Report 1984* (New York, NY: Oxford University Press, 1984).

124. "Power Shortages in Developing Countries: Magnitude, Impacts, Solutions, and the Role of the Private Sector," U.S. Agency for International Development, Washington, D.C., March 1988.

125. A.S. Miller, I.M. Mintzer, and S.H. Hoagland, *Growing Power: Bioenergy for Development and Industry* (Washington, D.C.: World Resources Institute, April 1986).

126. J. Goldemberg, T.B. Johansson, A.K.N. Reddy, and R.H. Williams, *Energy for Development* (Washington, D.C.: World Resources Institute, September 1987); H.S. Geller, "End-Use Electricity Conservation: Options for Developing Countries," Energy Department Paper No. 32, World Bank, Washington, D.C., October 1986.

127. H. Geller, et al., "Electricity Conservation in Brazil: Potential and Progress," *Energy, the International Journal*, 1988 (forthcoming).

128. "Power Shortages in Developing Countries."

129. Goldemberg, Johansson, Reddy, and Williams, *Energy for Development*.

130. "International Energy Outlook 1986," Energy Information Administration, U.S. Department of Energy, Washington, D.C., May 1987.

131. *The Energy Transition in Developing Countries* (Washington, D.C.: The World Bank, 1983).

132. "Foreign Operations, Export Financing, and Related programs Appropriations Bill, 1989," U.S. House of Representatives, Washington, D.C., May 19, 1988.

133. B. Rich, "Multilateral Development Banks, Environmental Policy, and the United States," *Ecology Law Quarterly*, Vol. 12, pp. 681-7, 1985.

134. J.R. Gamba, D.A. Caplin, and J.J. Mulckhuyse, *Industrial Energy Rationalization in Developing Countries* (Baltimore, MD: The World Bank and Johns Hopkins University Press, 1986).

135. H. Geller, et al., "Electricity Conservation in Brazil."

136. "Program Plan 1988-89," Office of Energy, U.S. Agency for International Development, Washington, D.C., 1988.

137. H.S. Geller, "Residential Equipment Efficiency: A State-of-the-Art Review"; H.S. Geller, "Commercial Building Equipment Efficiency: A State-of-the-Art Review"; R.H. Williams, E.D. Larson, and M.H. Ross, "Materials, Affluence, and Industrial Energy Use," *Annual Review of Energy* 12, pp. 99-144 (Palo Alto, CA: Annual Reviews, Inc., 1987); B. McNutt, "Oil Conservation Potential in the U.S. Economy," draft, Office of Policy, Planning and Analysis, U.S. Department of Energy, Washington, D.C., June 1988.

138. Energy Information Administration, "Annual Energy Outlook 1987," Washington, D.C., March 1988.